TARTUFFE

Molière

TARTUFFE

A translation by Ranjit Bolt

Introduction by Nicholas Dromgoole

OBERON BOOKS
LONDON

First published in this translation in 2002 by Oberon Books Ltd.
521 Caledonian Road, London N7 9RH
Tel: +44 (0) 20 7607 3637 / Fax: +44 (0) 20 7607 3629
e-mail: info@oberonbooks.com
www.oberonbooks.com

Reprinted in 2006, 2009, 2011, 2012

A catalogue record for this book is available from the British Library.

PB ISBN: 978-1-84002-260-5
E ISBN: 978-1-84943-575-8

Contents

Introduction

The first version of Molière's *Tartuffe* was performed in three acts at the royal court at Versailles on 12 May 1664, before the young Louis XIV. News of its contents provoked scandal, outrage and demands that the play be banned and Molière punished. As a result of intervention by the authorities it did not transfer to the expected public performance before a paying public in Paris. The literary world of the time seemed to flourish on vitriolic pamphlets denouncing every possible abuse, and *Tartuffe* certainly got its share. Molière was 'the devil come alive in a human frame'; the play 'committed *lèse majesté* against God and His Church.' What was going on? Was Molière an innocent playwright penning an amusing little comedy and quite unaware that he was blundering into a hornet's nest? Or was he a seasoned dramatist, well able to judge exactly the kind of publicity his subject matter would arouse, and how long queues at the box office could be summoned out of a public furore and outcry?

The days when the play was dynamite exploding into hates, fears and bitter prejudices have happily receded, and can really only be understood in the context of wider social issues of its own time. In the second half of the sixteenth century France nearly tore itself apart in a series of vicious religious wars between a Catholic majority and a Protestant minority. Beliefs were passionate and both sides totally committed, but there was another agenda. The growing power of the monarchy had eroded the status and privileges of the nobles, many of whom used the religious wars in a determined attempt to win back what they had lost. Fortunately for the monarchy, between 1630 and 1660 France had two remarkably able first ministers, Richelieu and then Mazarin, who both re-established and extended the King's power. The civil uprising of the Fronde in 1648 was the last despairing attempt to reverse this process, but it failed. From 1661 the young Louis XIV determined to rule France himself, without a first minister, and proved during his long reign to 1715 that he was one of the finest administrators France had ever had.

Catholicism in France gained renewed confidence and inspiration under thinkers like Cardinal de Bérulle, St Francis de Sales and St Vincent de Paul. A widespread movement called Gallicanism felt there was something special about French Catholicism, and opposed outside interference from the Pope in Rome. The rise of Jansenism, an extreme form of Catholicism, in many ways reflected this fresh energy and piety. On the other hand, Catholics undoubtedly felt threatened and insecure by growing Protestant zeal, and in Calvinism the Protestants had an extreme answer to Catholicism. Equally threatening was a growing revival of ancient Greek and Roman Stoicism among an educated minority, with its tendency to adopt a world-weary attitude to the theological disputes of the period: 'A plague on both your houses.' These attitudes are best exemplified in the writings of Guillaume du Vair and Pierre Charron whose *De La Sagesse* (1601) had a considerable influence, even extending to the Catholic brilliance of Blaise Pascal's *Pensées*.

Into this almost feverish atmosphere of renewed faith, energetic zeal and yet strange insecurity, with each side almost hysterically aware of enemies both without and within their respective camps, *Tartuffe* seemed to spearhead yet another attack. The play, like a red rag to a bull, infuriated the deeply religious. It tells of a rich man, Orgon, who takes a fake religious guru, Tartuffe, into his home, is seduced by his piety into offering him his daughter's hand in marriage and turning over his property to him, until the con-man is finally unmasked as a villain. Tartuffe repeatedly mouths high-sounding religious platitudes, and in creating a villain from this display of religious zeal, the play was bound to spark public uproar. It is safe to assume that Molière knew exactly what he was doing. But who was this seasoned playwright and where did he spring from?

Born in 1622, Molière's career in the theatre until his early death at fifty-one in 1673 divides neatly into two phases: humiliation and struggle for the first fifteen years, then increasing success and fame for the next fourteen years. His rich merchant family gave him the best education available, but he deserted the solid comforts of bourgeois family life to spend his entire career in the competitive rat race of the theatre. With a young group of fellow enthusiasts he set up a drama company, *L'Illustre Théâtre,* and bravely opened in Paris. There is no doubt he nursed delusions of grandeur. He saw himself, not only as a great tragic actor, but as someone who was going to revolutionise the conventional sing-song delivery of the tragic actors of his day. At this distance we have no idea of the rights and wrongs of his performance, but in the theatre, the audience is always judge and jury, and they would have none of these new-fangled attempts at tragic acting. The undoubted fact that Molière had an unfortunate stutter, particularly at moments of high drama and extreme emotion, cannot have helped.

Within two years his company was bankrupt and he was in prison for debt. When his father rallied and paid the debts, Molière, unrepentant, formed a fresh company, including the three members of the Béjart family who had joined him in setting up the original *L'Illustre Théâtre*, and disappeared into the provinces, to learn his trade the hard way, on tour for the next thirteen years. We would all like to know much more than we do about what he acted, what he wrote, but clearly during these years he learned how to be an actor, a playwright, a director, a theatre manager, a publicist and an ingenious manipulator of his fellow human beings. He was bright, massively well educated (he knew all the plays of Terence in Latin by heart), good-looking, charming, witty and fun to be with. He developed an outstanding talent as a comic actor, and became better and better at writing plays. It was only a matter of time before Paris discovered it needed him almost as much as he needed Paris.

In 1658 Molière and his company performed before the King at court. He must still have been nursing dreams of imposing himself as a great tragic actor. They opened with a Corneille tragedy, even though, in the audience, interested to see this provincial company about which they had doubtless already heard much, were members of the Bourgogne Company, famous in Paris for their tragic acting, presumably in the very style Molière was hoping to improve and supersede. Alas for innovation and change! The company and their tragedy were not well received. Fortunately Molière then saved the day by begging permission from the footlights to present a farce, written by himself, with himself in the leading role. It was an immediate success. The king was immensely amused. By royal command, Molière and his company were thenceforth installed in the *Salle du Bourbon* in Paris, sharing the premises with an Italian *commedia dell'arte* company, and each performing on alternate nights. The Italian company was directed by the famous Tiberio Fiorillo (*Scaramouche*), from whom in his younger days Molière had taken acting lessons. Hostile critics long taunted that most of Molière's best ideas were cribbed from the Italians.

Increasingly after that performance before the king in 1658, Molière became an influence in French cultural life. In a sense, he has never left Paris since 1658, and he is still very much a part of French thinking, indeed in any attempt to understand what being French involves, it would still be impossible to ignore Molière's contribution. This may seem a grand claim, but an even grander one can be made for him. France in the seventeenth century was at the heart of Europe's cultural life. French thinking dominated the ideology of the period, and French styles in clothing, manners and all the arts from architecture, painting and sculpture to literature, were imitated and copied all over Europe, potent symbols of France's domination of Europe at the time. Anyone lucky enough to see Roger Planchon's famous productions of *Tartuffe*, either in 1962, or the even more effective 1973 staging which, appropriately for what I am suggesting, opened in Buenos Aires, before coming to France (and was presented by the Planchon company at London's National Theatre in 1976), could hardly fail to realise that Molière is still not only French, but a treasured element of western culture as a whole. That is why he is so frequently translated into other languages and given so many productions outside France. Ranjit Bolt has happily caught much of the original's many-layered ambiguities and sheer sense of fun in the version for the Royal National Theatre published here.

It was no accident that when Molière first played before the King, he opened with a tragedy. When he arrived in Paris, tragedy reigned supreme. Humour was seen as a matter for broad farce or for the commedia. He chose a tragedy by Corneille, who had also written comedies, but even the *Oxford Companion to the Theatre* refers to Corneille as 'France's first great tragic dramatist'. Comedy was considered a lesser art. Molière greatly admired Corneille's comedy *Le Menteur* and is reported to have claimed that without it, 'I might have written *L'Etourdi* but never

Le Misanthrope.' But it was really Molière who gave comedy the same status in art as tragedy had previously enjoyed alone. Essentially it was his achievement as a writer, aided and abetted by his impressive gifts as an actor and a director. By creating recognisable characters in believable situations, he used humour to persuade his audience to confront many of the most important issues of his day. Because he was a creative artist, Molière was not happy just to repeat himself. Every play tackled something new, not just in its subject matter but often in its form as well. He repeatedly surprised his audience so that they never knew what to expect. Alongside ten one-act plays, a couple of Molière's plays have two acts, nine have three, and twelve have five. Each play fitted its subject like a glove. W B Yeats spoke of 'a theatre …joyful, fantastic, extravagant, whimsical, beautiful, resonant and altogether reckless.' Molière had already been there and done that.

Tartuffe, at its solitary first performance, was originally three acts, and Tartuffe may himself have been dressed in some form of holy orders. What was Molière trying to do?

Perhaps we should first remember that this was an amazingly conformist and conventional world. It was the last comfortable time in which nobody questioned the system itself. Here were the great majority of people working in relative poverty, crippled with taxes, in order to keep a small minority of aristocrats leading a life of idle luxury, hopping in and out of bed with each other at Versailles. Nobody asked if society could be organised on a fairer basis. Why on earth not? The answer is distressingly simple. This was a deeply religious age, and every body believed and accepted that God had ordained that there should be kings, nobles and peasants, and the good life consisted of making the best of whatever life God had allotted. Church and State mutually supported each other and upheld the status quo both ideologically and practically. To question the system was to question God, and as that unfortunate affair at Loudon was to show, there were still medieval punishments in store for anyone who dared to do that. Admittedly, across the Channel things were ordered differently. The English had been busily questioning the system for most of the century. They had beheaded their king and set up a Commonwealth, but the rest of Europe merely held up their hands in horror at what this rogue nation was up to. Just as Elizabethan drama had almost no effect on contemporary drama in France, so the ferment of revolutionary ideas in England was largely ignored by the French. It was not until the eighteenth century that the French started analysing what on earth had been happening in England. (And not until well into the nineteenth century that British drama made much of an impact on its chauvinist neighbour. Whereas the British had been slavishly copying French drama since Molière!)

Conformism had taken over the arts as well. Louis XIV established separate academies for architecture, for painting and sculpture, for music and even for dance, which laid down what was acceptable and what was not, and exactly how things should be done. The same rules were laid down for the decorative arts. We may feel today that our Serotas and our Arts Councils can occasionally seem to have too dictatorial a say in what is fashionable and acceptable and what is not, but conformism was much more greatly enforced in France under the Sun King. Literature, and particularly theatre, could not be so strictly controlled because patronage and commissions were less in the State's hands but rested far more in the Paris box office. Drama was more free to tackle what concerned its audience, not the authorities (but not if a furious Archbishop of Paris had anything to do with it).

Moreover, across the Channel in 1660, because England had grown fed up with Puritan austerity and, dare one say, hypocrisy, the Puritan Commonwealth had petered out, and Charles II had been invited back to reign over his people once again, and incidentally to allow theatre once more to flourish after it had been forbidden for a generation. Perhaps, like England, Molière and his Paris audience were fed up, not with piety, not with virtue, but with listening to hypocrites voice pious sentiments as a cover for much less admirable self-seeking.

It is possible too, for such are the vagaries of the creative impulse, that some of the force of the final *Tartuffe* may have arisen from Molière's bitterness towards Racine. In the same year as the first performance of *Tartuffe,* Molière's company was putting on a first play by a young man, all charm and intelligence, whom Molière had befriended, encouraged and brought into his literary circle. Through Molière, the young Jean Racine (1639-99) met writers like Boileau and La Fontaine. He also met the pretty women of Molière's company and started an affair with one of them: Mlle du Parc, even though she was apparently no stranger to the bed of Molière himself. Generously recognising the talents of someone younger than himself (both in the bedroom and on the stage), Molière not only advised Racine on his first play, *The Thebaid,* and produced it in his own theatre, but put on his second play, *Alexander the Great,* in 1665.

Racine had been brought up in a strictly Jansenist circle. This extreme form of Catholicism gave Racine an even bleaker view of life than most of his contemporaries. For Jansenists, man was not only born in sin, but was basically corrupt. Without God's grace to bolster the rather pathetic human longing for virtue and to stiffen the weak and wavering human will, the corruption of the flesh and the temptation of the world would triumph. Song and dance and theatre were all part of the world's insidious corruption. They trampled virtue and overcame the weak will. The young Racine, in joining Molière's circle and in writing plays himself, was consciously repudiating the beliefs he had been brought up in. No doubt he spoke about them with scorn. He too must have been sickened by the hypocrisy which a remarkably clever adolescent could discern in those ostensibly pious around him. Someone had already called Molière 'Dangerous! He carries his eyes and ears about with him everywhere!' Was it the young Racine's fulminations against his Jansenist upbringing that gave Molière the idea for *Tartuffe?* Worse was to come. As soon as *Alexander the Great* proved a success, Racine decamped with it to the Bourgogne Company. Shortly afterwards Mlle du Parc followed.

Molière could not believe such base ingratitude. He never spoke to Racine again and perhaps some of his fury and bitterness went into the final version of *Tartuffe?* Poor Mlle du Parc did not last long. When her charms faded for Racine, according to secret police reports, he murdered her to clear his bed for a more favoured competitor. And got away with it. In his case charm was only skin deep and the flesh corrupt indeed.

In spite of the wild protests from the clergy, *Tartuffe* the play is in no sense an attack on the Church. Nobody condemns Chaucer in his *Canterbury Tales* for including some pretty unsavoury characters among his clergymen, including a Pardoner who is clearly not going to be pardoned at all when he finally faces a stem St. Peter at the heavenly gates. Chaucer was exposing clergymen who did not live up to their vows, but he was not in any sense attacking the institution of the Church in his day, nor did his audience even remotely imagine he was attempting any such thing. It says a great deal about the subsequent sense of insecurity in the French Church that they were so quick to take offence when Molière did much the same as Chaucer. After that one performance at court in 1664, Molière presented a revised version in Paris in 1667. It was immediately banned after one public performance, and the Archbishop of Paris ordered that the play should be denounced from every parish pulpit in Paris. With hindsight, and gratefully with some of Roger Planchon's insight, we are better able to come to terms with the play today.

Unfriendly critics have attacked Molière because his characters do not develop. While they come vividly to life as recognisable individuals, they do not learn from experience and alter as they do so. They are what they are and they stay like that all through the play. Macbeth, Lear or Hamlet are very different men at the end of their plays from what they were at the beginning. Molière's characters are less like that. They are closer to Ben Jonson's 'humours' than they are to Shakespeare's individuals. Yet it is hardly a helpful criticism. There is not much point in belabouring Molière for not writing the kind of play a particular critic prefers. Molière's plays are about ideas. His gift was to embody these ideas in gloriously funny and believable people and to create ludicrous situations which allow these characters and the ideas they stand for to come into conflict with those around them. Planchon said that what he most liked about Molière was that his plays were not about individual personalities but about situations. Orgon in *Tartuffe* does not really learn anything. At the end of the play he is clearly going to be as fanatical about disliking the overtly religious as he has been fanatical about supporting them. Experience has not really altered him at all. The play is really about Orgon's tendency to get obsessed with his current enthusiasm, and his inability to see the effect this has on others. Molière himself acted the role of Orgon, not Tartuffe.

Whereas adultery had certainly provided subject matter for dramatic tragedies, as Planchon has pointed out, *Tartuffe* is the first French play to annexe adultery for comedy. Yet it is a very twisted kind of adultery. Orgon is bringing, not another woman to invade the closed circle of his family, but another man. And on the surface, his reasons have nothing to do with the physical or sensual world, on the contrary, it is because he wishes to be more saintly, more virtuous, that Orgon is in effect indulging in what in any other set of circumstances could only be seen as straightforward adultery. This immediately sets up a glorious array of comic contradictions. The family all behave just as they might if Orgon had fallen for a woman. They show the same resentment at this invasion of their family circle, and yet the ground is cut off beneath their feet. It is they who in normal circumstances should be wallowing in righteous and very moral indignation, and yet for them the righteous attitudes have all somehow been filched by the intruder!

The play is also about power: the power of money and a father's power in controlling his family. It has all the thrills and spills of watching how a criminal and gifted con-man, Tartuffe, gets his hands on the father's power, both his money, his daughter and, although foiled at last in the attempt, ultimately power over his wife. Tartuffe is wonderfully satisfying as a dramatic villain. There is the engaging difference between what he says and what he actually wants and achieves. Why does an audience so enjoy seeing the supposedly good and pious unmasked as being nothing of the kind? Why is Clinton misbehaving in the White House such good copy for the media, when red light districts in every city could provide much more lurid encounters?

Finally there is the last act, when just as the villain triumphs, almost as a god descending from the heavens, an all-seeing and an all-powerful monarch rights the wrongs, pardons Orgon for his foolish ways (he has strayed like a lost sheep) and punishes the wicked. Louis XIV had about as much power in a seventeenth century France, and in the play *Tartuffe*, as Creon has in Thebes in Sophocles' *Antigone*. Both are absolute rulers. The difference between the two audiences for these plays says much about western culture. Five centuries before the birth of Christ, the ancient Greek audience for Sophocles' play sat thanking its lucky stars that Athens was a democracy, and that tyrants like Creon were no longer permitted there. The seventeenth century French audience were all too aware of their king's very real power. It is only we, snugly ensconced in the twenty-first century, that can feel much as those Athenians did. Or can we? Parallels with an all-seeing, all-powerful state make us perhaps uncomfortably aware that in many ways we are closer to that seventeenth century French audience, and that Molière is still depressingly relevant. Social security officers can take away our children, security files may well have grossly inaccurate but damaging accounts of our activities, minor offences can give us a criminal record, our DNA is stored to be checked at any time. Paranoia? At least we are still able to empathise with Orgon, who has been pardoned this time – but perhaps the King may not be so understanding next time around.

Only after a painful elapse of time, and after two splendid petitions to the King from Molière, was the ban finally lifted and the play allowed to be performed in Paris in 1669. It was an instant success, and has since remained the most frequently performed of Molière's plays at the *Comédie Française*.

Nicholas Dromgoole
London, 2002

Characters

ORGON
a gentleman

MARIANE
his daughter

ELMIRE
his wife

DAMIS
his son

MME PERNELLE
his mother

CLEANTE
Elmire's brother

DORINE
their maid

VALERE
betrothed to Mariane

TARTUFFE
a religious fraud

LAURENT
his acolyte

MONSIEUR LOYAL
a bailiff

An OFFICER
of the court

FLIPOTE
Mme Pernelle's maid

This translation of *Tartuffe* was first performed at the Royal National Theatre on 23 February 2002, with the following cast:

MME PERNELLE, Margaret Tyzack

ORGON, David Threlfall

ELMIRE, Clare Holman

DAMIS, Tom Goodman-Hill

MARIANE, Melanie Clark Pullen

VALERE, Sam Troughton

CLEANTE, Julian Wadham

TARTUFFE, Martin Clunes

DORINE, Debra Gillett

MONSIEUR LOYAL, Nicholas Day

THE OFFICER, Martin Chamberlain

FLIPOTE, Marianne Morley

LAURENT, Scott Frazer

POLICEMEN, Andrew McDonald, Richard Hollis

KING LOUIS XIV, Nick Sampson

Other members of the cast:
Sarah Hay, Suzanne Heathcote, Deborah Winckles

Director, Lindsay Posner

Designer, Ashley Martin-Davis

Lighting Designer, Wolfgang Goebbel

Music, Gary Yershon

Director of Movement, Jane Gibson

Sound Designer, Christopher Shutt

Musicians, Mark Bousie, Walter Fabeck

ACT ONE

A room in Orgon's house. MME PERNELLE, ELMIRE, DAMIS, MARIANE, CLEANTE, DORINE, FLIPOTE.

MME PERNELLE: That's it. I'm leaving. Come, Flipote.
    My goat's been well and truly got.

ELMIRE: Please wait. We can't keep up with you.

MME PERNELLE: That's because *I* don't want you to.
    These antics chill me to the core.

ELMIRE: What do you have to rush off for?
    We show respect. You have your due.

MME PERNELLE: I'm horrified by all of you.
    I'm leaving in extreme distress –
    I've never liked this household less.
    Who listens to a word I say?
    Or does the smallest thing my way?
    It's more than I have strength to bear
    This chaos drives me to despair!
    When will you people ever learn
    To hold your tongues, or speak in turn,
    Respecting person, time, and place?
    Your slipshod ways are a disgrace!

DORINE: If –

MME PERNELLE: You're a servant, and as such,
    You tend to think, and talk, too much.
    When will your insolence be checked?
    When will you learn to show respect
    And not keep sticking in your oar?

DAMIS: But –

MME PERNELLE: *You* annoy me even more.
    You're nothing but a cloth-eared clot,
    I'm your grandmother, am I not?

I ought to know. You *were* a brat,
I often told your father that,
I warned him, too, what lay ahead:
'He'll be a constant cross,' I said.
'He'll cause you endless stress and strain.'

MARIANE: You want *my* view?

MME PERNELLE: Not *you* again!
    His sister – oh, you're *so* discreet,
    And butter-wouldn't-melt and sweet
    But you have cost me no less sleep:
    Still waters, as they say, run deep,
    Behind that smooth front, what goes on?
    The thought is a disturbing one.
    Devious – that's the word for you.

ELMIRE: But mother-in-law…

MME PERNELLE: I blame you, too.
    You are the stepmother from Hell,
    You don't do right, you don't live well,
    You're a *fine* model for these two!
    They *will* improve by copying *you!* –
    Their mother wasn't half as bad,
    Your spendthrift habits make me mad,
    Look how expensively you dress,
    You're got up *now* like some princess!
    A wife can't need such fripperies,
    There's nobody she has to please
    Besides her husband. That being so
    Why primp and prance, I'd like to know.

CLEANTE: But surely, in the present case…

MME PERNELLE: Her brother…yeees…you have a place
    In my esteem – I'm fond of you
    And sometimes share your point of view –
    I've heard you say things that were sane.
    And yet, to me, this much is plain:
    If my poor son had any nous

He would debar you from his house:
You stand on shaky moral ground,
The mode of life that you expound
Is one that no one should pursue –
No *decent* person, in my view.
Forgive my speaking as I find
But when there's something on my mind
I say just what I have to say
And mincing words is *not* my way.

DAMIS: Your friend *Tartuffe* would jump for joy...

MME PERNELLE: You should pay *him* more heed, my boy.
Tartuffe's a good man – no, the *best,*
And if there's one thing I detest
It is to see a *fool* like you
Carping at him the way you do.

DAMIS: The man is a censorious fraud
And yet he's treated like a lord!
He's seized control, that's what he's done –
No one can have an ounce of fun
Do *anything* but sleep and eat
Unless Tartuffe has 'deemed it meet'.

DORINE: Name just one thing he hasn't banned,
Condemned as 'sinful', out of hand –
We have some harmless pleasure planned
And straight off he prohibits it,
The pious, pompous, puffed-up git!

MME PERNELLE: How else are you to get to Heaven?
He *should* ban six things out of seven
And *you* should love him, all of you –
In fact, my son should force you to.

DAMIS: He couldn't, grandma. Nothing can
Alter my feelings for that man:
I hate him, and because I do
I say so: to thyself be true –
That's *my* creed. He enrages me

And, to be honest, I foresee
Dire trouble: I'll do something rash.
That swine and I are sure to clash.

DORINE: Who is he? No one seems to know.
That hasn't stopped him, has it, though?
He lords it over us, he does,
A guest? he bloody *governs* us!
He won't give over now he's parked
His big fat arse. He's got *me* narked.
I ask you, what was he before?
Apart from miserable and poor?
His clothes were worth about ten sous,
He wasn't even wearing shoes
But he's forgotten all that now –
Bossing us all about and...ow!

This, as MME PERNELLE hits her.

MME PERNELLE: If only what you said were true:
I wish he *had* control of you
And you obeyed his pious laws.

DORINE: He's pulled the wool right over *yours*
But *our* eyes see a hypocrite.
I wish you'd take my word for it –
Him and Laurent, his serving lad,
They're bad eggs both, *extremely* bad –
It scarcely needs to be discussed,
It's obvious: they're the kind you trust
No further than they can be thrown.

MME PERNELLE: How dare you take this bumptious tone!
The *servant* isn't my concern
And what he's like I've yet to learn –
I know the *master* through and through,
And *he's* a saint, I promise you.
This fierce hostility of yours
Springs from an all too obvious cause:
His censure makes you self-aware,
He lays your many failings bare –

But it's not you he's angry with,
It's sin itself he can't forgive,
So let him lecture and protest,
It's all in Heaven's interest.

DORINE: But what I still can't comprehend
Is why our sanctimonious friend
Will not allow us to receive.
What is he hoping to achieve
By forcing us to say we're out
And stopping people calling? Nowt.
Yet he makes such a song and dance.
You don't suppose, by any chance,
He's *jealous* – of Madame? Perhaps
The sight of her with other chaps
Is just too much for him to bear?
Yeeees, there's a whiff of something there.

MME PERNELLE: Why can't you hold your tongue, Dorine?
Your viewpoint isn't worth a bean.
You plunge straight in. You don't think first.
These visitors with which you're cursed,
The awful pother they create,
The constant coaches at your gate,
The servants with their dreadful racket,
No one who lives round here can hack it.
You say it's harmless fun. Maybe.
But people talk, which *worries* me.

CLEANTE: Oh, let them chatter – need we mind?
Wouldn't it be a dreadful bind
If nothing but a foolish fear
Of *gossip* kept us prisoners here,
Cut off from all our friends? What's more,
Suppose we *could* keep Tartuffe's law?
Tongues would still wag, it's what tongues do,
Scandal will find a passage through
No matter how secure a wall
We built against it – hang them all!
Their talk won't bother us a bit

As long as there's no grounds for it –
Provided we've done nothing wrong
They're free to babble all day long.

DORINE: Is it that blabbermouth Daphne?
The woman just across the way?
Her and her husband? Am I right?
They're slandering us, as well they might,
Since *they* are always talked about;
They're sniffing *other* scandal out,
Shame's not so shameful if it's shared,
Two sets of dirty sheets compared
Don't look as dirty as one set –
That's what's behind all this, I'll bet.

MME PERNELLE: That makes no difference, dunderhead!
What of Orante? She's always led
A pious life, a paragon
She is, or pretty close to one,
Her thoughts are fixed on God – and *she*
(So folk have been informing me)
Condemns this house, and execrates
The goings-on behind its gates.

DORINE: It's not a house that she'd condone,
Being an ancient, hideous crone.
It's age that's made that woman chaste,
And even if she *had* a taste
For sin, and hankered for a beau
(As well she may, for all I know)
Her *body* wouldn't play along:
She's not *equipped* for doing wrong.
She's knocked about, though, in her time –
You bet your life that, in her prime,
She put her...*points* to proper use.
But now her flesh is hanging loose,
She gets new wrinkles every day,
Her dazzling charms have ebbed away,
Skedaddled, never to return,
So what's she do? Pretends to spurn

A world that has in fact spurned *her*.
Her prudishness is, as it were,
Worn, like a sombre veil, to hide
A beauty that has putrefied.
Yes, she's austere, as well behoves
A woman men have left in droves.
Of course she criticises us.
What d'you expect? She's envious –
Of those who have *their* charms intact;
She seems so pious, but in fact
She's simply spoiling people's fun,
'Cos she, poor cow, is having none.

MME PERNELLE: What nonsense, girl!
   (*To ELMIRE.*)   You see, my dear,
The point that things have got to here?
No one's allowed to breathe a word
But Madam here. May I be heard?
May I, just this once, have my say?
I think it was a joyous day
When my poor son took in this sage,
This saint, this beacon for our age,
Whose coming Heaven has decreed
To save you in your hour of need,
Redeem your souls, and bring you back
Onto the straight and narrow track.
As for his strictures, I've no doubt
Such blame as he has meted out
Is earned. You ought, for your own good,
To pay him heed. I wish you would.
The social whirl, the idle chat,
The dinners, dances, all of that,
Are Satan's works. I can't recall
Hearing one pious word let fall
While in this house, just pure moonshine,
Waffle and gossip. You malign
Your neighbours, too – nobody's spared,
A war of words has been declared
On half of Paris. No one sane

Should come here, it infects the brain
To hear the din you people make,
The buzz of talk, for talk's own sake.
You know, in church the other day
A priest I know was moved to say
That parties, such as happen here,
These *routs,* give one a good idea
Of the old tower of Babylon,
For at them, people babble on.
Another parallel he drew –

She turns on CLEANTE, who is sniggering behind his hand.

I *won't* be tittered at by *you!*
Go find those silly friends you see
And laugh with *them,* but not *at me!*
(*To ELMIRE.*) Goodbye. I'm leaving. Don't you worry,
I shan't be back here in a hurry –
I've had my fill. Flipote, come on…

FLIPOTE has dozed off on her feet. MME PERNELLE hits her.

Well, *move,* you indolent moron!

She flounces out with FLIPOTE, followed anxiously by ELMIRE,
DAMIS and MARIANE. CLEANTE is about to go with them, then
thinks better of it.

CLEANTE: On second thoughts, I'm safer here.
    That mad old dragon's bent my ear
    Enough for one day.

DORINE: What's that? 'Old'?
    Oh, how she'd blast you, how she'd scold,
    If she could hear you call her that!
    There'd be the most almighty spat!

CLEANTE: These angry scenes she likes to stage?
    How *did* we put her in this rage?
    And also, can you tell me why
    Tartuffe's the apple of her eye?

DORINE: *Her* eye! You ought to see her son,
    He's really the besotted one.
    To think that he was taken for
    A wise man, in the civil war,
    A stalwart servant of the King –
    Does all that count for anything
    Now he's gone barmy? Does it heck!
    Tartuffe has got him at his beck
    And bloody call! Devoured him whole
    He has; possessed him, heart and soul.
    Become the centre of his life,
    Daughter and mother, son and wife?
    Forgotten for his new amour.
    Companion, confidant, mentor,
    Tartuffe is all of those in one.
    To see the way Monsieur Orgon
    Coddles him, and embraces him,
    And waits upon his every whim –
    A libertine could not adore
    His very favourite mistress more.
    At meals, the place of honour's his,
    No matter what the party is;
    The master sheds ecstatic tears
    Watching his darling, while he clears
    Dish after dish, plate after plate,
    More than Gargantua ever ate,
    And when he belches, with eyes raised,
    The master murmurs: 'God be praised!'
    He thinks the smallest thing he does
    Is more or less miraculous,
    If he broke wind he'd bottle it;
    He quotes from him like holy writ,
    Regards him as a…what's it called?

CLEANTE: An oracle. Well, I'm appalled.

DORINE: As for Tartuffe, he knows his man,
    He'll bleed him bloodless if he can,
    He's worked out how to keep him hooked,

No opening is overlooked –
He is performing, all the time,
A sort of pious pantomime
For which my master has to pay.
He gives him money. Every day
More of his gold is being poured
Into the purse of this fat fraud.
Sensing his power, Tartuffe grows bold,
His chief delight's to carp and scold
At all of us. His young valet,
Laurent, keeps entering the fray –
He'll fix us with his fiery eyes
And rant and rave and sermonise,
Or confiscate a beauty spot,
Ribbon, or rouge, or God knows what.
Just yesterday the little pest
Had found a kerchief being pressed
Between a book of martyrs' prayers.
''Tis mortal sin!' the boy declares,
'To place the Devil's fripperies
'Twixt sacred pages such as these!
This kerchief touches ladies'…heads!'
And then he tore the thing to shreds!

Enter ELMIRE, DAMIS, MARIANE.

ELMIRE: How wise to stay here! There was more –
A *second* lecture at the door.

Noises off: front door closing, ORGON's voice in the hall.

My husband! Can I face him? No.
I'll see him upstairs. Off I go.

Exit ELMIRE.

CLEANTE: I'll wait for him, and say Hello.
Though, there again, he's such a bore,
I can't think what I'm staying for.

DAMIS: My sister's marriage – don't forget –
You haven't spoken to him yet –

Tartuffe's against it – I suspect
That's why its progress has been checked:
He's planting doubts in father's head.
It's vital to me, as I've said,
That my old friend Valère should be
Allied, by marrying her, to me,
Since then his sister, whom I love…
I'm hoping that by virtue of…

DORINE: He's coming!

CLEANTE shoos DAMIS and MARIANE away. They go. ORGON enters, other side.

ORGON: Brother-in-law, good day.

CLEANTE: I was about to dash away.
It's good to have you back so soon.
So – countryside not quite in bloom?

ORGON: Dorine – (*Breaks off.*)
(*To CLEANTE.*)   Brother-in-law, no doubt
You understand, and aren't put out –
I must take each thing in its turn –
I've matters of more grave concern
To deal with first – I need to know
What's happened in my absence.
(*Turns back to DORINE.*)   So:
What *is* the news? How's everyone?
Is all well? What's been going on?

DORINE: The mistress gave us all a scare.
A fever came from God knows where
That had her rushing to her bed.

ORGON: And Tartuffe?

DORINE   Oh, his lips are red,
His mien is moist and fresh and sleek,
In fact his health is at its peak.

ORGON: Poor man!

29

DORINE: She suffered, that first night:
She seemed to lose her appetite.
The reason must have been the pain –
It was a *really bad migraine.*

ORGON: And Tartuffe?

DORINE: Oh, he ate and ate!
Sat by her with a piled-up plate
And very piously ploughed through
Two grouse, and lots of mincemeat, too.

ORGON: Poor man!

DORINE: She had a sleepless night,
The fever having reached its height –
We kept a vigil by her side.

ORGON: And Tartuffe?

DORINE: Once he'd satisfied
His appetite, he went to bed
And slept as soundly as the dead.

ORGON: Poor man!

DORINE: We kicked up such a fuss
She finally gave way to us
And let herself be purged and bled
Which knocked the fever on the head.

ORGON: And Tartuffe?

DORINE: He would not despair.
What must be borne, he meant to bear.
All blows he steadfastly withstood
And, to replace Madame's lost blood,
During his lunch the following day,
He put a quart of wine away.

ORGON: Poor man!

DORINE: They're both as right as rain:
He's still well, and she's well again.

If you'll excuse me, I must go:
I'm sure Madame would love to know
About your husbandly concern
And how relieved you were to learn
That hers were not a fatal case.

Exit DORINE.

CLEANTE: The girl was laughing in your face.
    With reason, too, I'm bound to say –
    Now, please don't take this the wrong way –
    But I don't think I've ever heard
    Of an obsession so absurd:
    How has it happened? How can *he*,
    Or any man, have this degree
    Of influence over you? Mere whim,
    That's what it is. You rescued him,
    You took him in, when he was poor,
    All well and good, but why do more?
    Why should you –

ORGON: May I stop you there?
    D'you know this man? Are you aware
    Of whom you're speaking?

CLEANTE: Maybe not,
    But certain *types* aren't hard to spot:
    I'd say Tartuffe was someone who…

ORGON: But if you knew him like I do
    You'd find him a complete delight –
    He is… Now let me get this right…
    He is a man… He *is* a *man*.
    Live by his doctrines – those who can
    Perceive this world but as a joke,
    Merely a whiff of conjuror's smoke.
    You know, Tartuffe's completely changed
    My view of life – he's rearranged
    My attitudes, and helped me find
    A true tranquillity of mind.
    Just talking to him's set me free:

31

I *needed* things – now I can see
It's all illusion, even love –
That's one disease he's cured me of:
Yes, I could see my family die
And not so much as blink an eye.

CLEANTE: Well, how humane.

ORGON: If you'd been there
When I first met the man, I swear
You'd have been captivated too.
Each day, in church, he'd take the pew
Right next to mine and, with an air
Of perfect meekness, kneel in prayer.
My God, what praying, though! What zeal!
A fervour one could touch, and feel!
The congregation gazed in awe
As now he stooped to kiss the floor,
Now heaved a heavy, pious sigh,
Or uttered a repentant cry.
Then, when I left, he'd go before,
Dash off to meet me at the door
And greet me with a splash or two
Of holy water. As to who,
And how *impoverished* he was,
I pretty soon found out, because
Laurent, his faithful acolyte,
Quickly informed me of his plight.
I gave him money after that,
Gifts he was always gibbing at:
'It's too much! Take back half,' he'd say,
'Don't throw your charity away
On such an undeserving one!'
I'd make him keep it, whereupon,
Not even caring if I saw,
He'd dole it out among the poor.
And then he came to share my roof.
God's will it was, and here's the proof:
I've prospered, *flourished*, since that day –

Everything seems to go my way,
And this, I'm sure, is the effect
Of being chivvied, chided, checked
By *him* – he sort of...*vets* one's life.
As for his interest in my *wife:*
You know, it almost equals mine!
He guards my honour all the time:
And thanks to him, if some young beau
Is ogling her, I'm sure to know;
He's *jealous* – yes, it really is
As if she weren't my wife, but his!
His zeal's the main thing – it's immense –
You know, he somehow seems to sense...
Can almost smell the stench of sin
In something *we'd* see nothing in!
And who is he the last to spare?
Himself. Last Tuesday, while at prayer,
He'd raised his hand to squash a flea,
And afterwards he came to me
Full of remorse, and pious pain,
Over this *midge* that he had slain!

CLEANTE: What utter rubbish! You're insane!
    You've buckled, from religious stress.
    Or are you joking? Please say yes.

ORGON: Brother-in-law that smacks of sin –
    I think you bear some spots within,
    If I were you I'd change my tune –
    Your soul will be in danger soon –
    I've warned you many times.

CLEANTE: Your kind
    All talk like that – because you're blind
    You'd rather others didn't see,
    You deem perceptiveness to be
    A kind of sin! Let us adore
    The idols that *you* kneel before
    Or else be damned! Well, listen here:

Your sermons don't fill *me* with fear:
I know my subject, for a start,
And Heaven sees into my heart.
I don't believe your pious pose.
If there's false courage, then, God knows,
There is false piety as well:
The brave man you can always tell
By how he doesn't rant and roar
And bluster, in the heat of war –
How may pious men be known?
They don't pull faces, sigh and groan.
D'you really have so dull a wit
That you can't tell a hypocrite
From an unfeigned, religious man?
It doesn't look as though you can –
You treat them as a single case,
Confound the visor with the face.
We humans are a curious lot –
The fact is, few of us have got
A sense of Nature's golden mean,
We can't keep straight, we have to lean
To one, extreme and dangerous side:
The bounds of reason aren't that wide,
Staying within them is a feat
Beyond our scope – you seldom meet
A man who'll tread its narrow way
If there's a chance for him to stray.
(That last bit wasn't *à propos* –
I felt I had to say it though.)

ORGON: Oh, you're infallible, you are!
    Nobody sees so deep or far –
    You are a Cato for our age
    An oracle, a mighty sage.
    Anyone else is just a prat
    Compared to you.

CLEANTE: I don't think that.
    But I know one thing more than you:

I *can* distinguish false from true:
Like the next man, I recognise
Religion as a thing to prize.
What jewel more precious can there be
Than perfect, unfeigned piety,
A fervour that is felt, and real?
But this…this *squashed flea* kind of zeal,
Worn, as a lady wears her paint,
The posturing of the plaster saint,
This, above all things, I deplore –
Nothing on earth disgusts me more
Than the religious charlatan,
The ladder-climbing holy man,
Whose sanctimonious grimace
Is *donned*, to get some post or place.
He's full of pride, ambition, spite,
Yet no one dresses wrong as right,
Or worldliness as sanctity
With greater stealth and skill than he.
He is more greatly to be feared
Because his weapons are revered,
His fervour's popular, and so
You will hear people cry, 'Bravo!'
As victims perish in the fire
Of his 'just' wrath, his 'righteous' ire.
But if you seek another kind,
The truly saintly, you will find
They, too, are easy to discern:
They do not seethe, and boil, and burn
With faith that's *too* good to be true,
They hate that sort of ballyhoo.
Nor will you see them rush about
Ferreting so-called sinners out
And damning them – they call that proud,
By them, some licence is allowed,
Humanity shines out of them,
There's only one way they'll condemn
Such actions as they can't condone –
That's by the goodness of their own.

Is your man like them? I fear not.
I'd lump him with the other lot.

ORGON: Thanks, brother-in-law. Now, is that it?

CLEANTE: I just mean he's a hypocrite.

ORGON: Good day, then.

CLEANTE: Wait! Let's leave it there
And talk of other things – Valère,
You chose him as your son-in-law,
You've given him your word, what's more.

ORGON: I have.

CLEANTE: You've named a day.

ORGON: Quite so.

CLEANTE: Why put it off?

ORGON: Damned if *I* know.

CLEANTE: Well…have you changed your mind?

ORGON: Maybe.

CLEANTE: You're going to break your word?

ORGON: Who? Me?

CLEANTE: But what on earth's preventing you?
There are no obstacles.

ORGON: Says who?

CLEANTE: For God's sake, can't you just be clear?
Valère himself has sent me here
To put his case.

ORGON: Well, praise the Lord.

CLEANTE: Look: *are* you going to keep your word?
Just *what* am I to *tell Valère?*

ORGON: Quite honestly, I don't much care.

CLEANTE: He has to know what you intend.

ORGON: To do God's will.

CLEANTE: But in the end
    You'll keep your promise? Yes or no?

ORGON: Goodbye.

Exit ORGON.

CLEANTE: Is this a fatal blow
    To Valère's hopes? A gruesome thought!
    I'd better give him my report.

Exit CLEANTE.

End of Act One.

ACT TWO

A room in Orgon's house. ORGON, MARIANE.

ORGON: Mariane!

MARIANE: Papa?

ORGON: I want a word –
   Here, where we can't be overheard.

He is checking a cupboard.

MARIANE: What are you looking for?

ORGON: For spies –
   The rooms round here have ears and eyes.
   That seems alright. Well now, my child,
   You are, by nature, sweet and mild,
   If you're my favourite, then that's why.

MARIANE: I've shown I'm grateful, haven't I?
   For all your love? I am, you know.

ORGON: Well said indeed, my child! Bravo!
   But it's a love that you must *earn:*
   By studying, at every turn,
   To make me happy.

MARIANE: So I do.
   My pride, my joy, is pleasing you.

ORGON: In such a child I'm truly blessed.
   Now tell me – how d'you like our guest?
   Tartuffe, I mean.

MARIANE: I'm sorry, I…

ORGON: Be sure to give the right reply.

MARIANE: Errmmmmm… Tell me what to say, papa.

ORGON: Well said, again! How wise you are!
Then tell me he's a paragon
That no one's virtues ever shone
So brightly; that your heart is his,
And that your dearest wish now is
That I bestow on him your hand.

MARIANE: Ummmmm…

ORGON: Well?

MARIANE: I don't quite understand…

ORGON: Pardon?

MARIANE: Did I mishear you?

ORGON: Eh?

MARIANE: Who is it I'm supposed to say…
Well, all of that?

ORGON: Tartuffe.

MARIANE: But why?
To tell you that would be to lie.
You're asking me to lie to you?

ORGON: No! I require it to be true.
I want you married to Tartuffe.
My wanting it should be enough.

MARIANE: You want Tartuffe…?

ORGON: My chief desire,
The thing to which I most aspire,
Is that this marvellous man should be
A member of my family.
Your heart is mine to give away
Or to withhold. You have no say.
You'll like it and… Good God! Dorine!

He has opened the door and DORINE has fallen into the room.

(*To DORINE.*) Hanging about! What does this mean?

What were you doing at this door?
Eavesdropping? You've been warned before!

DORINE: I don't know what it's all about –
  Just idle chatter, I've no doubt –
  Word of this marriage reached my ears
  But, Christ, of all the daft ideas!
  What rumour-mongers people are!

ORGON: Oh? Is the notion so bizarre?

DORINE: Is it bizarre? he says! And how!
  I heard you mention it just now
  And still I can't believe it's true.

ORGON: Oh, really? Well, you soon will do.

DORINE: No, it's a joke, and *you're* a tease.

ORGON: You'll soon see otherwise.

DORINE: Oh, please!

ORGON: (*Getting angry.*) It's *not* a *joke.*

DORINE: Oh, Mariane,
  He's such a scallywag, this man –
  It's all a big charade, is this –

ORGON: Now, look…

DORINE: Just playing games, he is.

ORGON: I tell you straight –

DORINE: You talk away –
  I won't believe a word you say.

ORGON: I'm getting angry…

DORINE: Alright, then,
  Have it your way – we'll start again:
  You're reckoned wise, you are, revered,
  What with your long, sagacious beard,

You're telling me you really mean...?
Oh, leave it out!

ORGON: Look here, Dorine,
This tone you take is far too free –
You can't think how it *angers* me!

DORINE: Calm down, monsieur. Let's talk it through.
No need to let it rattle you.
Now is this plan, this marriage plot
Simply some joke of yours, or what?
This girl is made of finer stuff
Than to be fobbed off with Tartuffe.
(The big fat bigot!) Let him keep
To higher things (the pious creep).
His bedroom should be used to *pray*
And not in any other way!
What would you want to choose *him* for?
He'd make a *rotten* son-in-law –
I mean, you're rich, and he's dirt poor.

ORGON: His poverty is what I prize –
It elevates him, in my eyes,
It does him honour, of a sort
No rich and powerful man at court
Could merit. But he's fallen prey
To frauds, who've sucked his wealth away,
And why? Because his pious gaze
Is fixed on Heaven, and he pays
Scant heed to things that have no worth –
The aims and objects of this earth.
He's now in pretty desperate straits,
But there are various estates
To which he has a legal claim,
In fact the deeds are in his name,
I'm going to help him get them back.

DORINE: Estates indeed! That doesn't smack
Much of *unworldliness* to me –
Shouldn't *unworldly* people be
Above such things as titles, birth,

'The aims and objects of this earth'
To use your phrase – ambition, pride…
Oo, heck! You do look mortified!
Alright, then, let's forget all that,
Say it's the *man* we're looking at –
Doesn't it trouble you to think
Of forging such a cock-eyed link?
A man like him, a girl like her?
I mean, who *wouldn't* she prefer?
You have to think what lies ahead:
Look, when a lass is made to wed
Against her wish, the risk is great
That some day she will deviate
From the straight path – d'you catch my drift?
Her virtue, God's most precious gift,
Is put in danger. In the end
Her moral conduct will depend
Upon the type of man she weds –
Some flowers belong in different beds –
When you see cuckolds pointed out
Just think what caused their horns to sprout,
They've *made* their wives the way they are,
Some husbands are a natural bar
To constancy. The lass will stray,
As surely as night follows day.
She'll frazzle in the fires of Hell
And you'll be packed off there as well,
For being such a bloody fool
And breaking Cupid's card'nal rule.

ORGON: Are you presuming to advise?
Is this your *counsel*, damn your eyes?

DORINE: You could do worse than follow it.

ORGON: She's talking like a rank halfwit.
Let's just ignore her, Mariane.
You *will* not find a better man –
Your father knows what's best for you –
I gave Valère my word, it's true,

For one thing, though, he's not averse
To *gambling* – and there may be worse –
The boy could be a *libertine* –
I can't think when he last was seen
In *church*, but it was months ago.

DORINE: And when's the lad supposed to go?
At your appointed times, is it?
With every other hypocrite
Who only goes so people see.

ORGON: Look here: your views don't interest me!
(*To MARIANE.*) Think how they differ on that score:
Nobody pleases Heaven more
Than Tartuffe – and that's *wealth*, alright –
No *earthly* treasure shines so bright.
As piety. It will be bliss
Living with him – consider this:
Each happy day, each *joyous* night
Brimful of pleasure and delight,
A pair of human turtle doves,
Forging two perfect, mutual loves
Into a single, happy whole!
Nor will time take its usual toll
Of acrimony and dispute
Whatever life you want, he'll suit.

DORINE: He'll suit a pair of *horns*, alright –
She'll cuckold him!

ORGON: *Will you be quiet!*

DORINE: It's *written* on him, can't you see?
'*Somebody's going to cuckold me!*'
In great big letters. It's his fate!
He won't escape it, sir – you wait,
No matter if the girl is chaste,
It's just a fact that must be faced.

ORGON: God, but you're getting in my hair!
Silence! This isn't your affair!

During the next interchange, DORINE keeps interrupting ORGON just as he is about to speak.

DORINE: I've got your interests at heart.

ORGON: I'll see to them – *you* needn't start.

DORINE: I love you, or I wouldn't speak.

ORGON: Your love's not needed, nor's your cheek.

DORINE: I'm to stop loving you, am I?
    I won't!

ORGON: My God!

DORINE: I won't stand by,
    While your good name goes up the spout,
    And you are mocked and pointed out
    By half of…

ORGON: Have you finished now?

DORINE: I simply can't and won't allow
    This cursèd marriage to occur!
    My conscience won't permit it, sir.

ORGON: What impudence! For Heaven's sake
    Shut up, you hissing, spitting snake!

DORINE: You're fuming. Are you sure you ought?
    You're meant to be a pious sort.

ORGON: My bile is boiling up in me,
    Heated by your stupidity!
    Not one more word will I allow,
    You really must stop talking *now!*

DORINE: Alright, I'll keep my mouth tight shut.
    I'll still be thinking thoughts, though, but…

ORGON: By all means think them, that's your choice,
    Just don't give any of them voice
    Or I shall…

He controls himself, and turns to MARIANE.

My decision's made,
And it's been very carefully weighed:
I've sized things up, and in my view...

DORINE: I've got to speak, I'm bursting to!

She shuts up as soon as ORGON turns round and gives her a look.

ORGON: (*To MARIANE.*)
Tartuffe's no young buck. Nonetheless
He's *framed* in such a way...

DORINE: Oo, yes!
A handsome mug and no mistake.

ORGON: That even if his virtues make...
No difference to you...

He turns and faces DORINE, arms folded.

DORINE: What a catch!
If *I* was forced into a match
I'd cast about, and find some way
To make my wretched husband pay.
Still warm, the wedding meats would be
When I began to let him see
How far a wife's revenge can go –
All women have their methods.

ORGON: So:
You're just ignoring what I've said!

DORINE: It's alright, don't go seeing red,
Those words were not addressed to you.

ORGON: Then just who *were* you talking to?

DORINE: Myself.

ORGON: My God, she's pushing it!
In fact, she's asking to be hit.

He gets ready to hit her. Whenever he looks at her she stands there, motionless and silent.

(*To MARIANE.*) Alright, my child, you know my mind...
You must obey me...and you'll find...
The man I've cho– you must agree...
(*Turns to DORINE.*) Eh? What? No more soliloquy?
No further comment? Not a peep?
Ideas run out? Tongue gone to sleep?

DORINE: I've nothing more to say to me.

ORGON: Go on!

DORINE: He's not *my* cup of tea.

ORGON: I knew you'd speak!

DORINE: The girl's a nit.

ORGON: (*To MARIANE.*) You'll simply have to live with it.
    This is the man you're ear-marked for.
    You're having him. My word is law.

DORINE: (*Running off.*) *I* wouldn't have him, not in *jest!*

ORGON: (*To MARIANE.*) My dear, your maid's become a pest,
    She is the enemy within.
    She'll cause me to commit a sin.
    Such insolence! It heats my brain.
    Enough. We'll speak of this again.
    But now I've got to get some air.
    I need to simmer down – out there.

Exit ORGON. DORINE comes back.

DORINE: I had to speak for you. How come?
    Had you been suddenly struck dumb?
    You let him set his mad plan out
    While *you* said what? Precisely nowt!

MARIANE: Oppose my father? In that mood?
    Fat chance. You saw his attitude –
    He's always so convinced he's right.

46

DORINE: You're up against it! You must *fight!*

MARIANE: How?

DORINE: You can tell him, for a start,
    That he does not control your heart:
    Who's to be married? Him or you?
    Who must the groom be pleasing to?
    He thinks Tartuffe's the 'best of men'?
    Let him get married to him, then!

MARIANE: My father's power over me
    Is such, I dare not disagree,
    Or even speak.

DORINE: Let's think this through:
    We know Valère's in love with you –
    The only problem we've still got
    Is whether *you* love *him* or not.

MARIANE: Dorine, that simply isn't fair!
    You know that I *adore* Valère,
    I've told you countless times.

DORINE: I know.
    You mightn't quite have meant it, though.
    You love him, then? With all your heart?
    You're not just acting out a part?

MARIANE: I've spoken from the heart throughout
    And I resent this sudden doubt.

DORINE: You love the boy?

MARIANE: With such a flame
    It sears me!

DORINE: And he feels the same?

MARIANE: Of course.

DORINE: You're set on getting wed?
    You wouldn't want Tartuffe instead?

MARIANE: I'll never be that monster's bride.
No, it's Valère, or suicide!

DORINE: Suicide! Brilliant idea!
Yes, once you're dead you're in the clear!
That's the best thought you've ever had!
(*Snapping out of sarcasm.*)
You talk such *tosh!* It makes me mad.

MARIANE: I'm staring into the abyss
And yet you harry me like this!

DORINE: I have to, when you go all limp
And blather like a witless wimp.

MARIANE: I'm timid. It's the way I'm made.

DORINE: Love can't afford to be afraid.

MARIANE: By staying faithful to Valère.
I'm trying to fight. And *he's* nowhere!
Why, surely, as the man, he's meant
To go and get papa's consent.

DORINE: Is he? A fat help that'd be:
Your dad's gone barmy, hasn't he?
A mad Tartuffomaniac
Who gives his word, then takes it back,
That's him! And yet you blame Valère!

MARIANE: Yes, but a *woman* can't declare,
Openly, that she loves a man,
And to oppose papa's new plan,
Refuse Tartuffe, reject him flat,
Is tantamount to doing that –
How long before the whole world knew?
Then there's my filial duty, too –
Valère would die for me, I know,
But *duty*, modesty –

DORINE: Quite so!
Alright, let's drop it, enough said,

Tartuffe has clearly turned your head,
I won't be standing in your way,
You snap him up without delay,
I've looked at him through biased eyes –
On second thoughts, he's quite a prize –
There's not a better man in France,
You nab him, while you've got the chance!
Madame Tartuffe – an envied rôle,
This is the man they all extol,
He's really an aristocrat.
(In his home town they call him that.)
He's handsome, too – no, no, he *is*,
What with those big red ears of his,
That face, as ruddy as a rose,
That massive, no, *majestic* nose –
These are not things at which to sneeze –
This is a moment you must seize.

MARIANE: Oh, God!

DORINE: You'll be the happiest wife,
    With Tartuffe, day and night, for life!

MARIANE: Stop it, Dorine! You're torturing me!
    Prevent this wedding! Hear my plea!
    I have no help on earth but you –
    Please! *Save* me! Tell me what to do
    And I will do it, come what may.

DORINE: Your father's spoken – you'll obey.
    Marry a monkey, if need be.
    It'll be Heaven. Wait and see.
    You'll take a coach to his home town
    Which will be teeming, overgrown
    With relatives – dozens and dozens
    Of lovely uncles, aunts, and cousins.
    Now, there's a prospect to enthral,
    You'll love it when they come to call,
    Then there'll be calls for *you* to pay,
    On all the smart set. Who are they?

Well, there's the bailiff's wife, the mayor's
(Coffee and cakes in comfy chairs)
Then there'll be dancing, at the fair –
There'd be some music, wouldn't there?
They're bound to have some bagpipes, no?
And don't forget the puppet show,
Ah! Punch and Judy – what delight!
Though, there again, your husband might…

MARIANE: You'll kill me! Please, devise some plan
　　　To rescue me from this *vile* man!

DORINE: No.

MARIANE:　　Please!

DORINE:　　　　　You've earned him, I'm afraid,
　　　I won't be coming to your aid.

MARIANE: But…

DORINE:　　　Uh-uh.

MARIANE:　　　　　　But I've told you straight…

DORINE: Sorry. You must accept your fate.

MARIANE: You can't abandon me, Dorine!
　　　For Heaven's sake, you've always been
　　　The loyal companion at my side
　　　When…

DORINE:　　You're to be Tartuffified.

MARIANE: Alright, then, since you just don't care,
　　　Abandon me to my despair,
　　　Despair itself will rescue me,
　　　Supply the surest remedy!

She is going.

DORINE: Where are you off to? Come back here!

MARIANE obeys, DORINE softens.

I may have been a mite severe.
I can't help pitying your plight.

We'll find a way to put things right.
No need for torment and despair.
We'll sort it out. Here comes Valère.

MARIANE: I mean it, though: I'll have to die –
What choice is there, if he and I...

Enter VALERE.

VALERE: (*To MARIANE.*) Madame, I cannot but enthuse
Over this marvellous piece of news.

MARIANE: What news?

VALERE: Your latest marriage plan –
I'm told Tartuffe is now the man.

MARIANE: My father does have something planned –
He means to give Tartuffe my hand...

VALERE: He does?

MARIANE: He's changed his mind.

VALERE: He's what?

MARIANE: He's just informed me.

VALERE: Surely not!

MARIANE: Tartuffe's his choice.

VALERE: What about you?
You're telling me he's your choice too?

MARIANE: I don't know...

VALERE: That's a nice reply!

MARIANE: What would you counsel?

VALERE: What would *I?!*
Oh, marry him!

MARIANE: That's your advice?

51

VALERE: Yes. Snap him up, at any price.
    He'll be a feather in your cap!

MARIANE: You mean that?

VALERE: Yes.

MARIANE: Then up I'll snap!

VALERE: Without a qualm, it would appear!

MARIANE: Don't start on *me!* It's *your* idea!

VALERE: But it's advice you hoped to hear.

MARIANE: I'll take him – if it pleases *you.*

DORINE: (*Aside.*) Let's see where this is leading to.

VALERE: So much for *your* love! All along
    I thought you meant it – I was wrong.

MARIANE: Don't speak of that, please. *Your* advice
    Was 'snap him up at any price'
    And that's what I intend to do.
    Thank you for counselling me to.

VALERE: Don't try and play *that* devious game
    And lumber *me* with all the blame –
    You've obviously made up your mind –
    You want him, and you'll never find
    Any excuse for what you've done –
    You broke a vow, a sacred one.

MARIANE: Quite so! You're absolutely right!

VALERE: My hold on you was very slight.
    You never really cared for me.

MARIANE: You're free to think so.

VALERE: You'll soon see
    Treachery's a game that *two* can play:
    There's plenty more fish, as they say.

MARIANE: Fish you can catch, I have no doubt.

VALERE: I'm nothing to write home about.
    I couldn't keep *you* on the hook.
    (*Darkly again.*) *However*, I know where to look
    For *someone* who'll accept me, who
    Won't mind that I've been *spurned* by *you*,
    Who'll soothe, redeem, console…

MARIANE: Console!
    Good! Excellent! You're still heart-whole.
    And soon you will have found a mate,
    One who will *more* than compensate.

VALERE: I'm going to have a damned good try,
    On that, Madame, you can rely.
    When we're rejected, our sole aim
    Must be to mitigate the shame,
    Purge the embarrassment away,
    Find a new girl, without delay.
    The worst thing is to hang about,
    Pining for one who's chucked us out.
    And if we don't achieve our end
    We must, for honour's sake, pretend.
    The man who doesn't is a fool.

MARIANE: Well said, Monsieur. A noble rule!

VALERE: Well, what am I supposed to do,
    Go to my grave in love with *you?*
    Never pursue a girl again
    While you *cavort* with other men?

MARIANE: No, no, pursue one. Please. Feel free.
    Start now. It's not too soon for me.

VALERE: You're *keen* that I should…?

MARIANE: Yes. I am.

VALERE: You've scoffed at me enough, Madame.
    I'll do your bidding. Off I go.

MARIANE: Who's stopping you?

He takes a step to leave, but keeps coming back.

VALERE: Remember, though,
There's really nothing I want less,
I'm acting on *your* orders.

MARIANE: Yes.

VALERE: Following your example.

MARIANE: Fine.

VALERE: Alright, then, I'll waste no more time.
You'll have your wish at once.

MARIANE: Oh, good.

VALERE: I just want one thing understood:
This is for life. For good and all.

MARIANE: About time.

VALERE: Hmm?

MARIANE: What?

VALERE: Did you call?

MARIANE: You're hearing things.

VALERE: Then I must fly.
Don't follow me… Madame – goodbye.

MARIANE: Goodbye, Monsieur.

DORINE: Are you both cracked?
It's daft, is this, and that's a fact!
I would have interrupted you –
I only left it till I knew
How far you'd go… Monsieur Valère!

VALERE: What do you want?

DORINE: Just stop right there!

She grabs his arm, he pretends to make a great effort to get away.

VALERE: No, no, I'm leaving. It's too late.
   I've got to find another mate.
   It's what she wants. You heard her.

DORINE: Wait!

MARIANE: Perhaps *I'd* better go instead.
   I'll only drive him off his head
   If I stay here. (*Going.*)

DORINE lets go of VALERE and grabs hold of MARIANE.

DORINE: Come back!

MARIANE: Let go!

DORINE: Come back this instant!

MARIANE: No, no, no,
   You won't persuade me to remain.

VALERE: My presence causes her such pain
   I'll go, and rid her of a pest.

DORINE: You put my patience to the test!
   Stop this and come back, both of you.

VALERE: What for?

MARIANE: What are you going to do?

DORINE: Sort the whole muddle *out* somehow,
   So drop this stupid quarrel *now!*

VALERE: You heard her. She was *very* rude.

DORINE: I don't defend her attitude.

MARIANE: As if *he* wasn't rude to *me!*

DORINE: I'm sick of both, quite honestly.
   Now, let me make this crystal clear:
   (*To VALERE.*) Mariane loves you, do you hear?
   (*To MARIANE.*) Valère completely dotes on you.

MARIANE: Then why did he advise me to…?

VALERE: Why did she *need* advice from me
    On such a subject?

DORINE: Honestly!
    You're mad, the pair of you. Come here.
    Give me your hands please. You too, dear.

VALERE: (*Giving her his hand.*)
    What for?

MARIANE: (*Giving her hers.*) What good's this going to do?

DORINE: Sweet Jesus! If you only knew
    How deep in love you are.

VALERE: Since when?
    (*To MARIANE.*) She had to *grab* your hand just then,
    You're looking at me *now* with hate!

DORINE: (*Aside.*) Beyond all question, I can state
    That lovers are completely mad!

VALERE: (*To MARIANE.*) Don't say I had no cause. I had.
    The callous way you broke the news!
    That, for a start, you can't excuse.

MARIANE: What about you? You've been a brute!
    Is that a charge you can refute?

DORINE: Look, can we just let all this bile
    Cool down and settle for a while?
    We have to stop this marriage. Now:
    Let's just keep calm and work out how.

MARIANE: Alright, then, tell us: what's the plan?

DORINE: Use every crafty ruse we can.
    Your father's clearly gone insane
    The Tartuffe bug has got his brain –
    Rather than have him using force,
    For now, I think your safest course,
    Is to pretend to play along –
    That way, if all our schemes go wrong,

There'll still be scope for some delay:
How d'you postpone a wedding day?
Well, obviously, there's no end
Of strategies – you could pretend
To suddenly have fallen ill,
Had magpies on your windowsill,
Or seen a ghost, or dreamed a dream,
And variations on that theme.
Meanwhile, it's not a good idea
For your papa to find *him* here (*Indicates VALERE.*)
Consorting with you.
(*To VALERE.*)   Right, dear: shoo!
The master made a pledge to you,
You've got a handle on him there,
Start bringing influence to bear,
Enlist your friends –
(*To MARIANE.*)   I should have thought
We'll get your stepmother's support,
Then there's your crazy brother too –
We'll have to see what *he* can do.

VALERE: (*To DORINE.*) We'll leave no avenue untried –
My God, I'm glad you're on our side!

MARIANE: (*To VALERE.*) My father may have fixed his course
But I'm not changing mine: I'm yours!
Yours unto death!

VALERE: What boundless bliss!
No earthly joy approaching this...

DORINE: Sssshhhh! Why must lovers chatter so?

VALERE: Whatever they...

DORINE: For God's sake, go!

VALERE: Whatever they're conniving at...

DORINE: *Go!* You through this door, you through that!

She pushes them off in different directions.

End of Act Two.

ACT THREE

A room in Orgon's house. DORINE, DAMIS.

DAMIS: I'll ward off this catastrophe.
    If anything should hinder me
    Let all France brand me as a clot,
    Or lightning strike me on the spot!

DORINE: You're too worked up by half, you are.
    What has your father *done*, so far?
    It's all hot air, a scheme, a thought
    That twenty thousand things could thwart.

DAMIS: I'll stop his plot in mid-career
    A friendly word in *Tartuffe's* ear,
    That's what's re–

DORINE: Steady as you go!
    There's still your stepmother, you know –
    Tartuffe might well be swayed by her.
    I think he's smitten – if he were,
    We'd practically be home and dry.
    She's asked to meet him here.

DAMIS: Oh? Why?

DORINE: To wheedle from him what she can
    About his thoughts on Mariane –
    This marriage that's upset you so –
    She'll *gauge* how far he means to go,
    And also try to make him see
    What repercussions there could be
    If he decided to pursue
    The course your father wants him to.
    His valet says he's still upstairs,
    Finishing off his morning prayers,
    But he'll be down soon. Disappear!
    Go on! I'll wait for him down here.

DAMIS: I'm witnessing this interview.

DORINE: Oh, no you're not – be off with you!

DAMIS: I'll keep my mouth shut – promise.

DORINE: No.
  It's him and her. Now off you go!
  Your temper carries you away,
  You'll only wreck things if you stay.

DAMIS: I'll be as good as gold, I swear.
  Won't even speak – I'll just be there.

  (*We hear* TARTUFFE's *voice, off.*)

DORINE: I've had it up to here with you!
  Heck! I can hear him coming! Shoo!

  She pushes DAMIS *off.*

  Enter TARTUFFE, *with* LAURENT.

TARTUFFE: (*He has seen* DORINE. *To* LAURENT.)
  My hairshirt may need wringing out,
  Also my scourge, Laurent. No doubt,
  When that is done, you'll wish to pray.
  If anybody wants me, say
  I'm at the prison.

LAURENT: What to do?

TARTUFFE: Just doling out my final sous.

DORINE: (*Aside.*) What an affected fraud he is!

TARTUFFE: (*To* DORINE.)
  What do you want?

DORINE: (*Coming forward.*) A word.

TARTUFFE: (*Gives her his handkerchief.*) Use this!

DORINE: Pardon?

TARTUFFE: Your *bosom's* well-nigh bare!
It *wounds* the soul, it's Satan's snare,
Engendering sinful thoughts, so, please,
Cover your improprieties!

DORINE: You mean two measly breasts can wreak
Such havoc? Is your flesh so weak?
Your blood so turbulent and hot?
Well, *mine* is definitely not:
Take you for instance: you could be
Completely nude, right next to me,
Just reams and reams of naked skin
And I'd have *no* desire to sin.

TARTUFFE: Be pure of speech, Dorine, I pray,
Or must I leave the room?

DORINE: No, stay.
I'm going – all I had to say
Is that *Madame* would like a chat
If you can spare the time for that.
She's coming down.

TARTUFFE: A talk with *her?*
Gladly!

DORINE: (*Aside.*) He's changed his pious tune –
He's all but gone into a swoon –
He loves her, then. So now we know.
I said as much an hour ago,
And I was right.

TARTUFFE: Will she be long?

DORINE: (*Aside.*) Na, fuck me sideways if I'm wrong.

Noise off, of ELMIRE on stairs.

Ah! Do I hear her now? I do.
I think it's high time I withdrew.

Exit DORINE by one door, enter ELMIRE by another.

TARTUFFE: Through the Lord's bounty, may you find

Good health, of body and of mind,
And Heaven bless you every way
As I, its humble servant, pray.

ELMIRE: Thanks for that pious wish. But please,
Let's sit – we might be more at ease.

TARTUFFE: I hope I find you well at last!

ELMIRE: A nasty fever, but it passed.

TARTUFFE: Can I have worked upon God's will?
I've been at prayer since you fell ill.
Have *I* restored your health, Madame,
Base, undeserving though I am
Of Heaven's grace?

ELMIRE: What pains you take!
And all for *my* unworthy sake.
You waste your precious zeal on me.

TARTUFFE: Not so, Madame – no pains could be
Too great in such a cherished cause –
I'd gladly trade my health for yours.

ELMIRE: This is a debt I dare not owe –
Too good, too kind, too Christian.

TARTUFFE: No!
It's *less* than you deserve, by far.

ELMIRE: Well, we're alone. I'm glad we are.
You see, I've something to discuss,
Strictly between the two of us...

TARTUFFE: Yes, we're alone, and I'm glad too,
It's like...like tasting honeydew,
I have been praying day and night
For this occasion, this *delight*
But only now has Heaven seen fit
To hear my prayer, and answer it.

ELMIRE: I need you to be frank with me.

TARTUFFE: This is my chance to let you see
    Into my soul, and read my heart,
    I *must* speak, all pretence apart,
    About the visits you receive,
    Over the which I often grieve:
    If I make bold to criticise,
    Know that the reason for it lies
    Not in some grudge I bear you – no,
    Not hatred, though it might seem so –
    The one emotion that I feel
    Is pure, unsullied, fervent *zeal* –
    I *yearn...*

ELMIRE: For my salvation, yes.
    That much I've not been slow to guess.

He clasps her hand, squeezing it violently in his.

TARTUFFE: This *ardour's* more than I can stand –

ELMIRE: Don't squeeze so hard! You'll squash my hand!

TARTUFFE: My *zeal,* excessive *zeal* again!
    I'd rather die than cause you pain.
    (*He has his hand on her knee now.*)
    Oh, God, what torture it would be...

ELMIRE: What's your hand doing on my knee?

TARTUFFE: Feeling your dress. One couldn't wish
    For softer silk.

ELMIRE: I'm ticklish!

She moves her chair away, but he moves his up to her again. He examines the lace round her bosom.

TARTUFFE: What splendid lace! The work's so fine!
    One of the marvels of our time
    Is Brussels lace, of course – but this –
    A masterpiece.

ELMIRE: You're right, it is.
    About this other matter, though:

There's something I should like to know –
A worrying rumour I've just heard –
My husband means to break his word,
That is, give Mariane to you
And not Valère. Can it be true?

TARTUFFE: He's hinted. I could not care less.
That's not where *I* seek happiness.
Can beauty move me? If it can,
It isn't found in Mariane –

ELMIRE: Meaning that you have soared above
Things *earthly*, and reserve your love
For higher, *heavenly* objects.

TARTUFFE: Oh?
My heart's not made of stone, you know –
There are two kinds of love – one springs
From contact with eternal things.
But that can easily comport
With passions of a temporal sort:
God's works enthral me, and therefore,
Madame, I cannot but adore
A lovely creature such as you –
You are a sheet on which He drew
His very image, which inspires
More… *ardent* feelings, nay, desires.
At first, they frightened me: maybe
Satan himself was tempting me,
In his familiar, devious fashion,
Through you. I wrestled with my passion,
I fought it back for my soul's sake,
As if salvation were at stake,
I was resolved to shun your sight,
But then I thought: 'This can't be right!
This passion cannot but be pure.'
Then, oh, you wonder, I was sure
My soul was safe, and I was free
To love you unreservedly.
Of course, it's folly on my part

To offer you this *dross* my heart,
Reckless, absurd, and impudent,
But look how far *God's* bounty went –
Can yours be very far behind?
Such is the grace I hope to find –
Though none to my mean self be due
Yet, I may look for all from you.
My hope, my happiness, my peace
Begin with you, without you cease;
How is my pilgrimage to end?
Upon your *fiat* I depend
To be the happiest of men
Or wretchedest – pronounce it, then!

ELMIRE: Well! This has come as a surprise!
    So gallant! Wouldn't it be wise
    To steel your heart a little more?
    To weigh things carefully, before
    Adopting that audacious tone?
    I mean, your piety's well known.
    For you to form so bold a plan...

TARTUFFE: I'm pious, but I'm still a man.
    To glimpse your beauty is to fall,
    To lose oneself beyond recall,
    And when a heart is forced to yield,
    Reason gives up; it quits the field.
    You don't expect such words from me
    But I'm no saint, why should I be?
    You find this declaration strange?
    To change it, *you* will have to change –
    Become less lovely, less *divine.*
    (Ha! Tell the sun it shouldn't shine!)
    You were adored as soon as seen,
    Crowned, on the instant, as my queen,
    How desperately my poor heart fought,
    Yet, in no time, it was the sport
    Of that sweet face, those sparkling eyes,
    That dazzling beauty, which defies
    Description! Fasting, weeping, prayer

Could not prevent your triumph there.
Don't say you didn't realise,
See in my looks, hear in my sighs,
That I was yours? This speech confirms
What's *been expressed* in stronger terms.
If you will condescend to have
Some pity on your worthless slave,
If your…your *majesty* will deign
To stoop to such a lowly plane,
Then, glorious goddess, I shall prove
There's such a thing as boundless love –
A love, moreover, free from shame:
I pose no threat to your good name:
The lady-killers of the Court
Treat love as just another sport,
To puff and plume themselves about,
The woman falls, the word is out,
She's named to everyone they meet,
Thus are their *tongues* so indiscreet
They desecrate the altars where
Their *hearts* make sacrifice. Compare
These braggarts with another breed,
Silent and secretive, whose need
To boast of conquests is as small
As the young buck's to vaunt them all;
It's to this class that I belong.
With us, Madame, you can't go wrong,
Your honour's safe, since we abhor
What you, too, have a loathing for –
Scandal. In me, and in my kind,
If you accept us, what you'll find
Is love of which the world won't hear,
And pleasure unalloyed by fear.

ELMIRE: You're quite an orator – the best,
That was most cogently expressed.
Suppose I told my husband, though?
What's to prevent my doing so?
Ending your friendship, at a stroke?

TARTUFFE: I thought of that before I spoke:
    You are too gracious and too good –
    Punish my love? As if you would!
    Mortals will err while mortals live
    And so will goddesses forgive.
    You want excuses for my pass?
    You'll find them in your looking glass.
    I'm *human* – who would you despise
    For having flesh and blood and eyes?

ELMIRE: Well, I *won't* tell him. Others might.
    This favour, though, you must requite:
    You're to do everything you can
    To help Valère and Mariane,
    Promote their marriage, and refrain
    From making others' loss your gain,
    Building your hopes on their despair.

DAMIS emerges from the cupboard, where he had hidden himself.

DAMIS: May I take issue with you there?
    I can't allow a compromise.
    We've got to open father's eyes.
    That's right: I overheard it all,
    From in there. *This* is what *I* call
    'God's bounty'. Oh, I'm truly blessed!
    Heaven has let me purge this pest!
    Vengeance is mine today! Hoorah!
    Proud, insolent trickster that you are,
    At last I'm going to make you pay
    And put your crimes on full display:
    Make love to her, you hypocrite?
    Wait till my father hears of it!

ELMIRE: I've let him off. Please leave him be.
    He'll mend. Let that suffice, Damis.
    If he deserves it, I'll be kind
    And keep my word. I'm not inclined
    To trigger off an ugly scene.
    A wife is wooed – who hasn't been?

A woman finds such pranks absurd
And sees no need to breathe a word
Or cause her husband great distress
Over what couldn't matter less.

DAMIS: I can't think why you should decide
To keep this back and save his hide –
You find it practical, no doubt –
Well bugger that! I'm speaking out.
We can't allow him to escape,
The fraudulent, insolent, lecherous ape!
He comes here, makes our home his own,
Turns the whole household upside down,
Tricks father with his pious airs,
Threatens my marriage, and Valère's...
It makes me mad! I'd rather die
Than let this golden chance go by –
I won't be deaf when vengeance calls –
Not now I've got him by the...

ELMIRE: Wait!

DAMIS: (*Ignoring her.*) Not now my bliss is at its height,
It's satisfaction, now, outright,
Or never. Nothing you can say
Will change my purpose. Come what may,
I'm acting, without more ado –
And here's my father, bang on cue!

Enter ORGON.

Father, you're going to find this news
As hard to credit as excuse:
Your doting love has been repaid
In somewhat false coin, I'm afraid:
Tartuffe's just tried to bed your wife.
You know she likes a quiet life,
She'd made her mind up not to tell,
She tried to silence *me* as well,
To do so would be wronging you,
Let blame alight where blame is due!

ELMIRE: There are more serious things, God knows,
    With which to wreck a man's repose:
    Was honour threatened, in the end?
    Am I not able to defend
    Myself against such impudence?
    Such are my craven sentiments,
    But you would not be swayed by me –
    I *wish* you'd held your tongue, Damis.

Exit ELMIRE.

ORGON: Well, I'm astonished. (*To TARTUFFE.*) Is this true?

TARTUFFE: Why should I try to hoodwink you?
    Brother, your son speaks true: I *am*
    A sinner, yea, a *wicked* man!
    My rank iniquities are rife
    And every instant of my life
    Is foul with sin! Yes, all the time
    I add another heinous crime
    To a long list. I roll among
    The other swine in swathes of dung!
    Small wonder Heaven is content
    To sit and watch my punishment.
    Whatever charge he wants to lay,
    Nothing, not one word, will I say
    In my defence – I lack the *pride.*
    Let me be loathed and vilified.
    Believe him! Give your wrath full rein!
    Cast me into the street again
    Like any felon. Shame? Disgrace?
    I merit them in any case,
    Lay ignominy at my door,
    I've *earned* it, fifty times and more!

ORGON: (*Rounds on DAMIS.*) You scheming rat! I see your game:
    You're trying to tarnish his good name
    With spurious crimes. This is a lie.

DAMIS: Don't tell me you were hoodwinked by
    That hypocritical charade!

ORGON: Silence, you dog!

TARTUFFE: (*To ORGON.*)   You are too hard!
    Let the boy speak. Believe him, too.
    Why shouldn't his account be true?
    Why favour *me?* What do you know?
    Tell me how far I might not go
    In wickedness. Brother, beware!
    You trust my outside, but what's there?
    What telling sign, what solid clue
    Says I'm the better of the two?
    Why should a cipher be believed?
    That's all I am, and *you're* deceived.
    You think I'm pious, *all* men do,
    But all I know, or ever knew,
    Is that I'm worthless. (*To DAMIS.*) Yes, my son,
    Pile up the charges, leave out none,
    Brand me a thief, a libertine,
    A fraud, a murderer, vent your spleen
    With yet worse names, accuse away,
    And not one charge will I gainsay,
    What reason have I to protest
    When they're the names that suit me best?
    Let me be execrated, spurned,
    Give me the shame that I have earned!

ORGON: (*To TARTUFFE.*) Brother, you're taking this too far!
    (*To DAMIS.*) Oh, what a treacherous beast you are!
    Have you no feeling? No remorse?

DAMIS: (*Disbelieving.*) You swallowed all that tripe, of course! –
    You did?! But, father...

ORGON: *Wretch*, no more!
    (*To TARTUFFE.*) Rise, brother!
    (*To DAMIS.*)   Rotten to the core,
    That's what you are.

DAMIS: But how can he...?

ORGON: *Silence!*

DAMIS: But are you telling me...?

ORGON: Silence I say!

DAMIS: To have to bear
Such vile...

ORGON: You'd better leave it there –
Or shall I snap your arms in two?

TARTUFFE: (*To ORGON.*) Peace, brother, peace, I beg of you.
Don't harm a hair on this boy's head
On my account. Hurt *me* instead.
Break *my* arms.

ORGON: (*To DAMIS.*) Monster!

TARTUFFE: Leave him be!
I'm begging you, on bended knee,
Forgive him!

ORGON: How can I do that?
(*To DAMIS.*) You see his saintliness, you brat?

DAMIS: You mean you...?

ORGON: Silence!

DAMIS: But...

ORGON: For shame!
You act with such an obvious aim:
You hate him, don't you, all of you?
Wife, children, maid, the whole damned crew,
You *must* destroy him, you will use
Any sly plot or shameless ruse
To do him down, and get him out.
Look at him, pious and devout,
Just look at him! You chew on this:
If that's your aim, you're sure to miss:
The more you work with that idea
The more I mean to keep him here,
And give my daughter to him, too,
And thwart and foil the lot of you!

DAMIS: You'll force this *fiend* on Mariane?

ORGON: I will, as quickly as I can,
    If possible, this very night,
    From sheer paternal rage and spite!
    I'm going to make you people see:
    The master in this house is *me!*
    Now, on your knees, at once, you swine,
    Beg his forgiveness – it's high time.

DAMIS: What! Beg forgiveness of that cur?

ORGON: Eh? What was that? Another slur?
    A stick, a stick! (*To TARTUFFE.*) Don't hold me back –
    (*To DAMIS.*) Out of my house, you maniac!
    Out! Now! Forever!

DAMIS: One thing, though –
    I'll leave, but…

ORGON: If you're leaving, go!
    I've cut you off without a sou –
    My *curse* is all I'm giving you!

    Exit DAMIS.

    Unutterable insolence!

TARTUFFE: Sweet Heaven, pardon his offence!
    They'll sunder us from one another
    With their malicious slanders, brother.
    Oh, how their lies have wounded me!
    To think of it is agony…

ORGON: Poor man! Poor man!

TARTUFFE: …a living death!
    I choke – I faint – I gasp for breath –
    I cannot speak –

    *ORGON goes to the door through which he has just driven DAMIS
    out and shouts after him.*

ORGON: You…you great wen!
I should have killed you, there and then!
(*He comes back to TARTUFFE.*)
Brother, for God's sake, you must rest,
You're shaken, battered and distressed.

TARTUFFE: It's obvious that I'm the cause
Of these absurd domestic wars.
If we're to bring them to an end
I'll have to leave your house, my friend.

ORGON: What? Leave? You're mad!

TARTUFFE: I'm hated here,
They're plotting, and their aim is clear:
To make you think that I'm a fraud.

ORGON: Who cares, if what they say's ignored?

TARTUFFE: But they'll persist. They'll chip away.
The slanders you reject today
Will, in due course, be listened to.

ORGON: Not till the sky has fallen through!

TARTUFFE: A woman's hold upon her spouse
Is strong…

ORGON: No!

TARTUFFE: Let me leave your house.
For then what sallies can they make?

ORGON: No, brother! Stay! My life's at stake.

TARTUFFE: Then, I'll endure their cruelty,
But, if and when you turn from me…

ORGON: *Ah!*

TARTUFFE: *Fiat sic!* We'll say no more.
But one thing I *must* ask you for,
May I demand it, as your friend?
One favour, that will put an end

To gripe and grudge, that will forestall
Possible scandal (after all,
Honour is such a fragile thing) –
There must be no more *mingling*
Between me and your wife –

ORGON: No, no!
Be intimate with her, *more* so,
On that, I really must insist,
Let no occasion now be missed
To cause a stir! Let's have some fun!
Let's put the wind up everyone!
Be seen with Elmire night and day!
To get at them another way
I'm going to make you my sole heir –
Let them oppose me if they dare!
A deed of gift, that's what we need –
I'll *give* you all I own – agreed?
My closest friend, my son-in-law
You mean as much to me, no, *more*,
Than mother, daughter, wife – or son.
What do you say?

TARTUFFE: God's will be done!

ORGON: Poor man! I'm off to change my will.
The swines! This ought to make them ill!

End of Act Three.

ACT FOUR

A room in Orgon's house. A table, with a bottle of wine on it. TARTUFFE,
CLEANTE.

CLEANTE: I'm very glad I've found you here
    I want a quick word in your ear.
    It is the talk of half the town
    And, need I say, your stock's gone down.
    People aren't taking it too well –
    You're censured, *hated*, truth to tell.
    I won't examine this close to –
    Let's take a pessimistic view
    And call it all a calumny
    Devised with malice, by Damis:
    Still, it is better to forgo
    Vengeance than to exact it, no?
    Isn't that the Christian way?
    I'm sure it's what the scriptures say.
    Is Orgon to disown his son
    So you can see full justice done?
    You want to know what I'd advise?
    Make peace. Accept a compromise,
    Not tooth for tooth and eye for eye –
    Back down, forget it, let it lie,
    And use your influence with Orgon –
    Persuade him to take back his son.

TARTUFFE: I long for peace with all my heart,
    Were it permitted – for my part,
    I bear no grudge, I *love* Damis,
    But I'm afraid it cannot be.
    For *Heaven* will not have it so:
    If *he* returns, then I must go –
    How is it *meet* that I should stay
    When he has acted in this way?
    No, tongues would wag, the world would say
    That I was guilty, and afraid.

That, having done what he had said,
I wished to keep my enemy
As close as possible to me
To stop him saying anything.

CLEANTE: That's specious, spurious reasoning.
    'Heaven will not have it so'!
    And how the Devil would *you* know?
    That is the question we must ask:
    Would God assign to *you* the task
    Of punishing a guilty man?
    D'you loom so large in Heaven's plan?
    God's *mercy* – *mercy's* what we want,
    His wrath is quite irrelevant.
    Hasn't He told us to forgive?
    To turn a cheek? Live and let live?
    Do as he says then! Need you mind
    About the judgement of mankind
    When what you're called on to fulfil
    Is nothing less than Heaven's will?
    Of course not – if an action's good
    Who cares if it's misunderstood?
    Why give a damn what people say?
    Just do the right thing, come what may.

TARTUFFE: Forgive Damis? Of course I do!
    How could I not? God tells me to.
    But the disgraceful things he's said,
    The shame he's heaped upon my head,
    They are too much for me to bear –
    Heaven does not order me to share
    A *roof* with him.

CLEANTE: I see. And pray,
    Just what does Heaven have to say
    About this whimsical idea
    Orgon's just had – I'd love to hear.
    He means to make you his sole heir:
    Perhaps you have some scruples there?
    Or does Almighty God demand

That you take money, goods and land
That are not yours, or shouldn't be,
Because their owner's off his tree?

TARTUFFE: No one who knew me would maintain
That I'd done *anything* for gain,
If I've a vice, it isn't *greed:*
Money's the last thing I could need.
Earthly allurements leave me cold,
The glint of jewels, the gleam of gold
Don't dazzle me. And if I take
This gift his father wants to make
It's only out of *fear* – that's right,
An apprehension that it might
Fall into hands, the Lord knows whose,
That would not put it to good use,
That might wreak evil with such wealth,
Not, as I mean to do myself,
Distribute it among the poor,
Putting God's glory to the fore.

CLEANTE: What subtle fears you're troubled by!
What you should ask yourself is why
You're cheating Orgon's rightful heir.
If there is any danger there,
I mean, in this inheritance,
Then let the poor lad take his chance,
Let him possess what's his by right.
Will he abuse it? Well, he might.
It would be infinitely worse
If people thought you'd lined your purse
At his expense. This much is plain:
The holy scriptures don't contain
A single passage that declares:
'Thou shalt defraud thy neighbour's heirs'!
And as to sharing roofs, try this:
You're not a guest we're going to miss,
I certainly won't feel the lack –
You go, and let Damis come back.

He pauses to see how TARTUFFE *takes it; no reaction from him.*

This won't look good, believe you me...
Monsieur...

TARTUFFE: Monsieur, it's half past three.
I'm sorry, I must go upstairs
For more self-chastisement and prayers.

CLEANTE: (*Calling after* TARTUFFE, *who is leaving.*)
A pseudo-Christ, that's what you are!
When you were born, was there a star?
Did you rewrite Celestial Law?
And was this water here before?
(*Points at the bottle and glass with wine in it on the table.*)
Ah!

Enter DORINE, MARIANE, ELMIRE.

DORINE: Please, Monsieur, we need your aid,
The girl is fading, I'm afraid,
I fear she's lost the will to fight,
The contract's to be signed tonight,
Let's band together, you and I –
We simply must have one last try...
He's coming!

Enter ORGON, with a parchment in his hand.

ORGON: Everybody here?
(*To MARIANE.*) You know what this contains, my dear –
This contract here is nothing less
Than your long lease on happiness!

MARIANE: (*Kneeling.*) Father, I beg you, in the name
Of Heaven, who beholds my pain:
If, in your heart, I still excite
Some feeling, waive a father's right,
When you command, I must obey,
This once, don't exercise your sway.
For pity's sake, don't make me rue

The day that I was born, when *you*
Bestowed on me the gift of life.
Stop me from being Valère's wife,
Destroy my only hope of bliss,
But, please, content yourself with this,
Consider it as Hell enough,
Don't *add* the torment of Tartuffe!

ORGON: (*Feels himself weakening, and chivvies himself.*)
Stay firm! No human weakness, please!
Have to be tough at times like these.

MARIANE: Be kind to him, be far *too* kind,
Pamper, prefer him, I don't mind,
By all means, let him help himself
To hearth and home, to wife and wealth,
Add *my* wealth, too, to eke yours out –
My *body*, let him do without.
Let me become a nun instead,
Since all I wish to be is dead
Why should a *living* death dismay?

ORGON: That's an excuse to disobey:
A headstrong girl can't have the one
She wants, so she becomes a nun.
It's an old trick. The more you fight
The more convinced I am I'm right:
Your flesh must now be mortified
To curb your insolence and pride.
Some suffering's long overdue.
Get up!

DORINE: But hold on…

ORGON: Shut up, you!
I've instituted a new law
Which says you can't talk anymore.

CLEANTE: May *I* throw in my thruppence worth?

ORGON: *You* are the wisest man on earth –
I don't want wisdom, not today.

ELMIRE: Well, well! I don't know what to say.
    You're *still* so blind? This makes no sense,
    Considering today's events.
    Tartuffe has *really* turned your head –
    No, if you found him in my *bed*
    You're so besotted, so obsessed
    You'd just say: 'Splendid – be my guest.'!

ORGON: It's shaky ground *you're* standing on:
    You're biased, you support my son,
    And when he set his little snare
    You didn't speak, you didn't dare,
    But you were too controlled, too calm,
    You didn't show enough alarm;
    You lent no credit to his lie.

ELMIRE: I hadn't just been raped, had I?
    A woman's colour needn't rise
    Or fire be flashing in her eyes
    Over a little harmless pass;
    The man's attentions are a farce,
    I'm not some prude, forever keen
    To throw a fit and make a scene,
    Nor do I think it very wise
    To scratch out some poor fellow's eyes
    For uttering a salacious word!
    I find it equally absurd
    To splutter like a lunatic
    When one smart put-down does the trick?

ORGON: I know the facts. I'm sure I'm right.

ELMIRE: His lunacy has reached its height.
    (*To ORGON.*) Suppose I managed to arrange
    A *trap?* Would your opinion change?
    If we could catch him out? What then?

ORGON: A trap?

ELMIRE: Yes.

ORGON: Pish!

ELMIRE: But, if and when…
   An *in flagrante rendez-vous*
   Conducted in full view of you –
   You'll see him at it –

ORGON: Can't be done.

ELMIRE: But just suppose I *managed* one.
   It's hypothetical as yet
   But if this gin, this snare, was set,
   And you could see him, hear him, *then*
   Would he still be the best of men?

ORGON: I might… I might…but, as I say,
   You couldn't do it anyway.

ELMIRE: I don't like being accused of lies.
   I'll lift the scales now from your eyes.
   It's high time. Without more ado
   I'll prove that all we've said is true.

ORGON: Prove it? I'd like to see you try!
   Press on, then – I'll be standing by.

ELMIRE: (*To DORINE.*) Send for him.

DORINE: Ah, but he's so sly,
   You bet your life he'll smell a rat.

ELMIRE: Oh, yes? I wouldn't bank on that –
   He loves me, and he's also vain,
   That double drug will dull his brain –
   We'll catch him. Send him down.

   Exit DORINE.

   (*To CLEANTE and MARIANE.*)   You two,
   Skedaddle, please – I shan't need you.

   Exeunt CLEANTE and MARIANE. ELMIRE brings a table over.

   (*To ORGON.*) Get underneath this table, quick.

ORGON: What for?

ELMIRE: So I can play my trick.

ORGON: The table? But I fail to see...

ELMIRE: Look, will you just be ruled by me?
    Be patient. Soon you'll understand.
    I've got the whole thing neatly planned –
    Now come on, underneath you go –
    And keep well hidden.

ORGON: *I* don't know!
    I let myself be messed about –
    Still, have to see how this turns out.

ELMIRE: You won't regret it. – One thing more,
    Something I'd best prepare you for:
    In order to remove his mask
    I'll have to – say things. I must ask
    That you keep calm, and *quiet*, throughout.
    Remember what this is about –
    Uncovering a hypocrite –
    I'll have to lead him on a bit
    And let him think he has some hope,
    To hang himself he'll need some rope,
    No matter what you hear me say
    It's for your sake. And anyway
    To stop me, all you have to do
    Is show yourself – it's up to you
    How close we get, how far he goes,
    There'll be a moment, I suppose,
    When you, yes, even you, see sense
    And have sufficient evidence –
    I won't be called on to proceed...
    To go too far when there's no need.
    Well, anyway, I hope that's clear:
    A: risky though it may appear
    It's all being done for you, and B:
    It's in your power to rescue me.

    Noises off: TARTUFFE whistling a hymn.

(*Whispers.*) That'll be him. Take up your post.
Don't let him see you, or all's lost.

ORGON stows himself under the table; enter TARTUFFE.

TARTUFFE: You sent for me?

ELMIRE: I had a few
More…secrets to discuss with you.
Before we start, though, shut the door
And check, check carefully.

TARTUFFE: What for?

ELMIRE: Remember last time, and Damis – ?

TARTUFFE is checking the room.

You know, he really frightened me –
I was afraid for *you*, I mean –
My goodness, what a nasty scene!
The boy would not be pacified,
You saw yourself how hard I tried
To calm him, and to stop the leak –
I must admit, when he did speak,
I should have said it was a lie
But I was worked up, wasn't I?
I couldn't think straight. Anyway,
You're safe – all's well that ends well, eh?
My husband couldn't take against
A man he'd placed among the saints.
People will talk, they always do –
He'll thwart them, he's determined to –
Hence his insisting that you see
As much as possible of me!
That's useful: we can linger here
And talk, and…*dally*, without fear;
I can be bolder now, and start
To open up my amorous heart,
And hasten to reciprocate
Your love – or maybe I should wait…?

TARTUFFE: This morning cold, this afternoon
    So warm, nay, hot – *you've* changed your tune!

ELMIRE: You were upset by my rebuff?
    Why then, Monsieur, it's plain enough
    You don't know women, or the clues
    We give, the secret code we use:
    A love so falteringly denied,
    A heart so feebly fortified,
    I can't imagine where you've been
    If you don't fathom what they mean:
    Some small resistance we must make,
    If only for our honour's sake,
    No matter how sincere our love
    If there's one thing we're chary of
    It's telling all – we're made that way,
    But what we feel and what we say
    Are different things, and all the while,
    If we reject you in this style,
    It's clear we're really ripe for sin:
    We turn you down – you know you're in.
    There now, I've made my feelings known,
    A lot of reticence *I've* shown!
    But now I've spoken, don't you see?
    I wouldn't have restrained Damis,
    Or heard you out so patiently,
    Received the offer of your heart
    Without deterring you, from start
    To finish, acted, in a word,
    As you have seen, and felt, and heard,
    Unless I welcomed your advance...
    And here's another circumstance:
    Just why did I oppose this plan
    Of matching you with Mariane?
    What did you understand by that?
    What was I really driving at?
    Didn't that more or less declare:
    'I want you all, and not a share!'?

83

TARTUFFE: These words from *you*, the one I love,
  The woman I've been dreaming of,
  They course, like honey, though each vein,
  Never before, never again
  Have I, or will I, know a bliss,
  Or a pure sweetness such as this.
  For me your love spells happiness –
  I am – *mistrustful*, nonetheless:
  Why should you drop into my lap?
  How do I know it's not a trap?
  Let me be frank: I don't see why
  You wouldn't stoop to tell a lie,
  In fact, use every means you can
  To make me give up Mariane.
  This garden has a weed of doubt,
  It's up to you to root it out:
  What words affirm, let *actions* prove:
  You've spoken, now *enact* your love,
  Bestow some bounty on your slave –
  Give me a taste of what I crave.

ELMIRE: (*She coughs to alert her husband.*)
  Isn't it rather soon to start
  Extracting honey from my heart?
  That declaration cost me dear
  I had to overcome the fear
  That all my sex is subject to
  But that's not good enough for you
  And now you're rushing to the sweet
  Before we've had the soup and meat.

TARTUFFE: This blessing is a great deal more
  Than I deserve, Madame; therefore
  I daren't believe it's come to me.
  Words can't convince me, I must see
  And touch, and taste it – then I'll know,
  Even *my* confidence will grow,
  But till you've granted my desire
  I'll think it madness to aspire,

84

To one so far beyond my worth –
Like seeking paradise on earth.

ELMIRE: My! When there's something that you want
You're *frighteningly* adamant!
Your love exerts a brutal sway,
You're fiercer than a bird of prey
In your pursuit! There's no respite,
No breathing space. It can't be right
To *harry* helpless creatures thus,
Abuse the hold you have on us
In this uncompromising style.

TARTUFFE: Why won't you go the final mile?
You said you wanted me.

ELMIRE: I know.
Won't Heaven frown upon us, though?

TARTUFFE: Heaven an obstacle to love?
If so, it's one I can remove.

ELMIRE: I thought the ten commandments said...

TARTUFFE: Why are you bothering your head
With such inane concerns? Look here:
You haven't *anything* to fear,
God's outlawed certain pleasures, true,
But He grants dispensations, too,
Our conscience needn't be obeyed,
Exceptions can, and *should* be made.
To know if something is a sin
First ask what *mood* you did it in,
Was your *intention* pure, and sound?
If so, you must be on safe ground.
Simply accede to my desire,
Try to forget about hellfire,
And if you *are* wrong, giving in,
I'll take upon *myself* the sin
And make quite sure that you're let off –
My goodness, what a nasty cough!

ELMIRE: My chest's completely up the spout.

TARTUFFE: This liquorice juice'll sort it out.

ELMIRE: Oh, no, this phlegm is here to stay,
    No juice will make it go away.

TARTUFFE: How vexing.

ELMIRE: *Very* vexing, yes.

TARTUFFE: Well, Moses couldn't matter less,
    The ten commandments don't apply,
    There's no one here – just you and I,
    It's *scandal* that creates the sin,
    This won't get out, so let's begin.

ELMIRE coughs some more.

ELMIRE: It seems I've no alternative
    But to give in, so in I'll give –
    No stalling, no more argument,
    I'll simply yield, and be content.
    I'd have postponed our bliss a while,
    Such rampant haste is not my style,
    But the *consensus* seems to be
    That you should have your way with me,
    I've not been *taken at my word,*
    More concrete proofs are now preferred,
    I've put my case – at least I've tried
    But *others* won't be satisfied,
    So I won't fight them any more,
    I'll give them what they're *asking for.*
    If, in so doing, I commit
    A sin, you're right, the blame for it
    Must lie elsewhere – with those, in fact,
    Who *drove* me to this desperate act.

TARTUFFE: I'll take the blame. I said I would.
    The point is…

ELMIRE: Would you be so good
    As just to check the corridor?

It might be prudent, no? Before...
My husband might be lurking there...

TARTUFFE: What if he is, though? Should we care?
For Heaven's sake, he's even said
That we're to meet, the dunderhead!
Trust me – I lead him by the nose –
My power is such, I don't suppose
That if he walked in through that door
And found us naked on the floor
He would believe his own two eyes!

ELMIRE: I dare say – still, it might be wise
(Don't you agree?) to just pop out
And have a thorough sniff about.

Exit TARTUFFE; ORGON comes out from under the table.

ORGON: The man's a monster! You've destroyed
My world! What's left? A gaping void!

ELMIRE: What? Out already? Back you get!
You've not had evidence as yet.
Don't you rely on supposition!
Let the thing *come* to its fruition!

ORGON: No. He's a fiend. Straight out of Hell.

ELMIRE: Your doubt's too easy to dispel!
You'd made a stand. You mustn't yield.
Not till the truth has been revealed.
Don't form your judgements with such haste.
This new distrust could prove misplaced.

Re-enter TARTUFFE; ORGON hides behind his wife.

TARTUFFE: I've checked. I've hunted everywhere.
There's absolutely no one there.
Madame, now everything conspires
To crown my uttermost desires!
My soul is ra–

ORGON: (*Stopping him.*) Not *quite*, Monsieur
Your *zeal* has lost control, I fear.

I must say, I'd have thought a *saint*
Might exercise more self-restraint!
My, what a fool you've made of me!
My daughter wouldn't do, I see,
She couldn't sate your appetite,
You wondered if my wife just might!
I thought I'd make them change their tune,
Now I'm convinced, and none too soon,
I carried incredulity
To mad lengths. Now it's clear to me
That every word they've said is true.

ELMIRE: (*To TARTUFFE.*) Such are the lengths he drove me to.
It's not my nature to deceive.
He made me.

TARTUFFE: (*To ORGON.*) But you can't believe...

ORGON: No speeches, please. We've heard your last.

TARTUFFE: But I...

ORGON:　　　　　　　The time for talk is past.

TARTUFFE: But my intention was...

ORGON:　　　　　　　　　　　Just go...

TARTUFFE: But...

ORGON:　　　　　Leave this house directly!

TARTUFFE:　　　　　　　　　　No.
Why *should* I leave it? Why don't you?
These ruses you've resorted to
To finish with me – what's the point?
I'll put your nose well out of joint
You have no power to injure *me* –
I'll punish your hypocrisy.
While also righting Heaven's wrongs –
What? Leave this house, when it belongs
To *me?!*

Exit TARTUFFE.

ELMIRE: To *him?!* What *can* he mean?

ORGON: Oh, what an imbecile I've been!
    The deed of gift!

ELMIRE: The deed? What deed?

ORGON: Sweet Jesus! This is all we need!
    There's worse, though…

ELMIRE: Worse than what? What's wrong?

ORGON: Oh, you'll find out before too long.
    (*Beating his forehead with his fist.*)
    I've been an absolute moron!
    Now where's that cursèd casket gone?

End of Act Four.

ACT FIVE

A room in Orgon's house. ORGON, CLEANTE. ORGON is rushing about.

CLEANTE: Where are you going?

ORGON: I've no idea.

CLEANTE: So, how do we proceed from here?
    We ought to talk it over, eh?

ORGON: The casket fills me with dismay.
    The rest is nothing next to it.
    You'd think I would have had the wit...

CLEANTE: Do please explain this mystery.

ORGON: It was a trust, or meant to be,
    Left here by Argas, my old friend,
    He's gone, but on it may depend –
    Goodness, his life, his property...
    Before his exile, he chose me
    To guard it for him – documents –
    Incriminating evidence.

CLEANTE: And you did what with them...? Oh, no –
    You gave them to *Tartuffe?*

ORGON: 'Fraid so.
    The renegade, the traitor.

CLEANTE: Why?

ORGON: To have a sort of alibi,
    So if it came up, and the State
    Decided to investigate,
    In conscience, I could then declare
    I'd had no part in the affair,
    Which, while it isn't strictly true,
    Would do the trick and see me through.

Or such, at least, was Tartuffe's line.
I went and told the devious swine
And he persuaded me to place
The papers in his care – in case.

CLEANTE: It's not a *brilliant* hand you've played.
This, and the gift you went and made,
Forgive me, but they seem to me –
Ill-judged, Orgon – to a degree.
You've given him a hold on you,
And you've antagonised him, too –
Throwing him out was most unwise,
You should have sought a compromise.

ORGON: But to *dissemble* in that way!
A plaster saint, with feet of clay!
I put him on his feet again!
I've had it with religious men.
In fact I hate them, and henceforth
I'll hound the sods for all I'm worth!

CLEANTE: Now there you go again, you seem
Always to rush from one extreme
Straight to another. Seek the mean,
The prudent, proper, in between.
Your sense of balance goes awry
Repeatedly – I can't think why:
So, now, you come across *one* fraud
And straightaway, across the board,
All on the basis of *one* case
You postulate…

ORGON: Oh, shut yer face!

Enter DAMIS.

DAMIS: Well, father, *has* he made this threat?
Is there no limit he will set
To perfidy? And does he plan
To scupper and destroy the man
Who made him what he is?

ORGON: My son! –
  He has, he does, and no, there's none!

DAMIS: I'll crop his ears for him! Just wait!
  I'll *kill* the insolent ingrate!
  I'll do what any good son must
  And fell him with a single thrust!

CLEANTE: I would have said that, in my day,
  But, please, there *is* a middle way –
  Moderation, common sense,
  They cure our ills, not violence.
  Let's just keep calm and wait and see.

Enter MME PERNELLE, DORINE, MARIANE, ELMIRE.

MME PERNELLE: It's baffling! *What* a mystery!

ORGON: Ah, but I saw it. I was there.
  Some payment for my love and care!
  The man is desperately poor,
  I take him in (God knows what for),
  Become his brother, more or less,
  Heap him with favours and largesse,
  Bestow on him my daughter's hand,
  Nay, more than that, my house and land,
  I totally transform his life
  And then he tries to bed my wife!
  The scoundrel hasn't finished yet:
  On top of this, he makes a threat:
  To throw me out, to ruin me
  With my own generosity!
  Armed with advantages he got
  From *me*, he promptly forms a plot
  To crush me – treacherous and cruel,
  That's what he is – and I'm a fool!
  Talk about turn and turn about!
  I give the house – and get chucked out!
  I end up poor, he ends up rich,
  He's in my home, I'm in the ditch!

DORINE: Poor man!

MME PERNELLE: This simply can't be true.
Tartuffe behave like that? Pooh pooh!

ORGON: Would you mind saying that again?

MME PERNELLE: Envy's the fate of pious men.

ORGON: Mother, what *are* you trying to say?

MME PERNELLE: This house gets madder every day.
Tartuffe's the man they love to hate.

ORGON: I'm sorry, how does that relate
To what I've told you? Not at all.

MME PERNELLE: I taught you this when you were small:
The envious die, but envy won't.

ORGON: (*To the others.*) D'you find that relevant? I don't.

MME PERNELLE: It's all lies – stupid, spiteful lies.

ORGON: I *saw* him, damn it, with these eyes!

MME PERNELLE: No – slanderous tongues on every hand,
All poisonous talk.

ORGON: Well I'll be damned!
I *saw* him, *heard* him, in the act.

MME PERNELLE: Another saint is being attacked.
Against such slurs there's no defence.

ORGON: But what you're saying makes no sense:
I *saw* him, I keep telling you –
Saw – you know: S – A – W.
Christ, must I cram it in your ears?
Or yell at you for twenty years?

MME PERNELLE: Our ears deceive us all the time.

ORGON: Why is matricide a crime?

MME PERNELLE: Most people have suspicious minds
And one perpetually finds
The good mistaken for the bad.

ORGON: It was my wife he would have had.
  D'you think that would have been, in fact,
  Some sort of charitable act?

MME PERNELLE: You're quick to form these damning views.
  First get your *proof,* and then accuse.

ORGON: What further proof was needed then?
  Should I have only stopped him when...
  Should I have waited till he'd... Ah!
  Mother, you'll make me go too far.

MME PERNELLE: Tartuffe do such a thing? No, no,
  I'm sorry, but it can't be so.
  Don't try to lay this at his door –
  The man is *saintly* to the core.

ORGON: I'm miffed, I'm mad, I'm mortified!
  God, if you weren't my mother, I'd...

DORINE: (*To ORGON.*) She's totally incredulous
  Exactly like *you* were with *us.*

CLEANTE: Stop bickering, for Heaven's sake,
  Let's think what action we must take,
  The man has made a monstrous threat.
  We've not worked out our tactics yet.

DORINE: He's made a threat, but will he act?
  He'd have to be completely cracked!

ELMIRE: He can't intend to see it through.

CLEANTE: I hate to disillusion you...

ELMIRE: He's so ungrateful, then? So base?

CLEANTE: He'll give his crime a decent face –
  He'll win important people's trust
  And make them think his cause is just;
  Cabals and factions thrive that way,
  Trapping new victims every day
  Within their evil maze. (*To ORGON.*) Again,
  I have to say, to cross him, when

He had such weapons – oh, Orgon,
Why did you?

ORGON: Why would anyone?
I flipped my lid, I blew my top,
I started and I couldn't stop,
I mean, the man's infernal *pride*.

CLEANTE: We ought to leave no course untried.
You never know. I still have hope.
With luck there may as yet be scope
For some accord between you two.

ELMIRE: Needless to say, I never knew
He *had* these weapons. If I'd known
I would have left things well alone.
My...

A knock at the door.

ORGON: Who the devil can it be?
Dorine, shut up and go and see.

Exit DORINE.

How horrible, a visitor –
The last damned thing I'm ready for.

DORINE and MONSIEUR LOYAL in the vestibule.

MONSIEUR LOYAL: Good even'. Is thy master in?
I feign would have a word with him.

DORINE: There's nobody he wants to see.
He's got sufficient company.

MONSIEUR LOYAL: My visit's for his benefit.
I think you'll find he'll welcome it.

DORINE: Your name?

MONSIEUR LOYAL: It ought to be enough
To tell him that Monsieur Tartuffe
Has sent me here to do him ease.

DORINE: I'll go and tell him. Wait here, please.
(*She rejoins the others.*)
He's from Tartuffe. Seems friendly, though.

CLEANTE: Who is this man? We need to know.
What can he want? Let's have him in.

DORINE goes to fetch him.

ORGON: My manner – how should I begin?
Could be some sort of compromise.

CLEANTE: Amicable's what I'd advise:
Conciliate, don't antagonise,
Attend to what he has to say
And if it seems –

DORINE shows MONSIEUR LOYAL in.

MONSIEUR LOYAL: Monsieur, good day –
May Heaven speedily destroy
All those who work for your annoy
And rain down blessings on your head
To overflowing.

ORGON: (*Aside, to CLEANTE.*) As I said,
It *is* some sort of compromise!
Or why so friendly, otherwise?

MONSIEUR LOYAL: This house is dear to me, because
I served your father, when time was.

ORGON: Indeed? Monsieur, I must admit,
I really don't remember it,
Or even know your name.

MONSIEUR LOYAL: Quite right.
Loyal. I first beheld God's light
In Normandy. I humbly ply
The trade of *bailiff,* thus have I,
These thrice ten, long years, won my bread,
And honoured been, and prosperèd.
But now, if you will bear with me,
I have a writ to serve on thee.

ORGON: A writ? What writ? You mean to say...?

MONSIEUR LOYAL: Peace! Calm yourself, Monsieur, I pray.
'Tis but an order that you quit
Your house, that thou surrender it
To its new owner, presently –
Such chattels as pertain to thee
You keep, your house is forfeit, though.
You've no recourse, you needs must go...

ORGON: Hell's teeth!

MONSIEUR LOYAL: And in the following wise:
'Tis with Tartuffe the judgement lies,
This is his property, not thine,
In *his* hands, as this writ in mine,
It must be placed, by process due,
There's nothing you can say or do.
'Tis meet and fit.

DAMIS: Well, I must say!
(*Instantly apopleptic.*) We've seen some impudence today,
But *this* – !

MONSIEUR LOYAL: I have no truck with thee,
Why do you rant and rave at me?
This man is sweet and kind, and knows
That no good person must oppose
The course of justice. 'Twere not meet.

ORGON: But...

MONSIEUR LOYAL:
(*To ORGON.*)   You'll not bluster, Sir, or bleat,
But, as an honest man and true,
You'll let me serve this writ on you.

DAMIS: (*To MONSIEUR LOYAL.*)
I'll tan your blasted bailiff hide,
You stupid, fat, self-satisfied – !

MONSIEUR LOYAL: (*To ORGON.*)
    Sir, pray, command him to a peace
    Or else your woes will soon increase,
    For I myself shall summons thee
    In my own right.

OTHERS: Shut up, Damis!

MONSIEUR LOYAL: (*To ORGON.*)
    You're a good man. I knew you were.
    I undertook this charge, Monsieur,
    Out of pure love, to do thee ease
    And lighten thy calamities –
    Better a man that means no ill
    Than somebody who would, or will,
    Be much less courteous with thee.

ORGON: Courteous! You're evicting me
    From my own house!

MONSIEUR LOYAL: A brief delay
    Is granted thee. Tonight thou't stay
    Beneath this roof, and I with thee,
    And ten strong men to succour me.
    Thou must, before thou go'st to sleep
    Surrender me thy keys to keep,
    I'll see that none disturbs thy rest
    And order all things for the best.
    Upon the morrow, at first light,
    Thy leaving thou must expedite
    And void this house of its contents,
    My men will help thee bear them hence.
    I've kindly dealt with thee I trust
    As any man half human must
    And I conjure thee, use me well,
    Bear with me for a little spell,
    And let me do my job aright,
    For, if thou puttest up a fight,
    And try'st in ought to hinder me,
    Be warned, it shall go hard with thee.

ORGON: I'd sell off all my property
    And raise my very final sou
    To buy the right to cudgel you!

CLEANTE: Leave him. It's useless to resist.

DAMIS: It's time this fellow felt *my* fist!

DORINE: This bailiff's got a nice broad back,
    It's simply asking for a thwack,
    Now, where's a stick?

MONSIEUR LOYAL: (*To DORINE.*) Thou art a maid
    Right worthy to be stripped and flayed.

CLEANTE: Monsieur, there's nothing more to say.
    Give us the writ, and go away.

MONSIEUR LOYAL: (*Giving it to ORGON.*)
    May Heav'n defend, and keep thee well
    Till next we meet.

ORGON: Oh, go to Hell!

Exit MONSIEUR LOYAL.

(*To his mother.*) Erm, were you saying someone lied?

MME PERNELLE: I'm stunned, distraught and stupefied!

DORINE: Perhaps, since wealth corrupts the soul,
    Tartuffe is taking on the role
    Of wealthy man, which leaves you free
    To find God's grace: it's charity
    Is this!

ORGON: For the last time: be quiet!
    Silence is golden, you should try it!

CLEANTE: How *are* we to escape this hell?

ELMIRE: I still say things will turn out well –
    Once his ingratitude is known,
    Once the authorities are shown

How he has cheated, tricked and lied,
His claim will be disqualified –
It isn't over till it ends.

Enter VALERE.

VALERE: Monsieur, one of my closest friends,
    Who has a place at Court, and knew
    The ties connecting me to you,
    Despite his duty to the State,
    Has let the due procedures wait,
    Broken his vow of secrecy,
    And revealed certain facts to me:
    Facts that amount to one thing: flight –
    You must be out of France tonight.
    The scoundrel you've been harbouring
    Has just denounced you to the King;
    You're guilty of a grave offence,
    He's handed over documents
    That *prove* your guilt – that much is clear,
    What your crime *is*, I've no idea,
    But something to the vague effect
    That you've attempted to protect
    One of the State's worst enemies,
    And now it's *you* they mean to seize.
    My friend revealed to me, when pressed,
    That *he's* been charged with your arrest,
    He and his men are on their way.

CLEANTE: This was the ace he had to play.

ORGON: A fiend, a monster, and a swine!

VALERE: You mustn't talk, there isn't time.
    My coach is waiting at the door.
    Here is a purse of *louis d'or*
    For your immediate needs. Let's go.
    This is the sort of sudden blow
    That desperate steps are suited to –
    If you agree, I'll come with you
    And see you safely stowed away.

ORGON: Such kindness! Well, I shall repay
This debt to you, before I'm done.
Now, listen to me, everyone...

CLEANTE: Sorry to stop you in full flow,
But don't you think you'd better go?
We'll work out later what to do.

Enter TARTUFFE, with the OFFICER.

TARTUFFE: Monsieur, where are you rushing to?
Your carriage, and new home, await,
You are a guest now – of the State.

ORGON: So, have you left the best till now?
Is this the final, fatal blow?
You...!

TARTUFFE: Please – insult me, curse and swear,
Heaven will give me strength to bear
Your insolence.

CLEANTE: A saint indeed.

DAMIS: He mocks religion – that's his creed.

TARTUFFE: Not so. I'm giving Heaven its due.
By all means, hate me, all of you.

MARIANE: A truly pious enterprise.

TARTUFFE: My strength, my vindication lies
In the great *power* that sent me here.

ORGON: How can your conscience be so clear?
I rescued you from dire distress.

TARTUFFE: You were extremely helpful, yes,
But *duty* before everything
And mine must be: to serve my King;
All other obligations pale
Beside it; *him* I must not fail.

ELMIRE: You fraud!

DORINE: He wears his holiness
   As you or I might do a dress.

CLEANTE: (*To TARTUFFE.*) This *duty*, that you hold so dear –
   It's taken some time to appear –
   Why did it wait, till you'd been caught
   Chasing his wife? I should have thought,
   If his black crimes disgust you so,
   You'd have denounced him long ago.
   He also made you his sole heir,
   How could you feel no scruples there
   But just accept his kindnesses
   If he is what you say he is –
   A traitor?

TARTUFFE: Have you said your piece?
   Then let this contumely cease.
   (*To the OFFICER.*) Monsieur, if you would condescend –

OFFICER: Indeed, it's time to make an end,
   Let's do so, without more ado:
   (*To TARTUFFE.*) Monsieur, I am arresting you,
   Your cell and manacles await –
   You are a guest, now, of the State.

TARTUFFE: Who? Me?

OFFICER: Yes, you.

TARTUFFE: But on what ground?

OFFICER: That's not for your ears. It's been found.
   (*To ORGON.*) Monsieur, you're naturally dismayed,
   Perhaps it's time that I allayed
   Your fears: the King, our sovereign lord,
   Is the archenemy of *fraud:*
   He sees, with his all-piercing eye,
   Into a scoundrel's heart, thereby
   Foiling his guile and treachery.
   His is an all-perceiving soul,
   That views life steadily, and *whole,*
   Calm, never running to excess.
   He bestows honour and largesse

On the sincerely pious man,
But he *discerns* the charlatan,
Of every artful ruse aware,
Deftly avoiding every snare,
Love for the best among mankind
Has not, and will not, make him blind
To the deceptions of the worst:
Small wonder, then, that from the first,
When faced with this vile hypocrite,
His keen intelligence had hit
Upon the truth. No subtle art
Could hide the blackness of that heart:
Tartuffe denounced you, and he thought
He'd scuppered you, but he was caught
In his own trap. The King could sense,
With his sublime intelligence,
That here was an *impostor*, one,
Moreover, who, it seems, has done
Similar, wicked deeds elsewhere,
Under another name. A rare
Trickster, whose life of crime and fraud
Would take whole volumes to record.
Well, in a word, the King could see,
And he deplored, this perfidy,
Last in a *roll* of infamies.
Tartuffe requested that he seize
And dispossess you, he agreed,
Dispatched me to you, with all speed,
But just to trap him, and to show
How far his wickedness could go.
Your property is yours again,
All deeds that bear this traitor's name
Are now annulled, by royal decree,
And he is to resign to me
Your private papers –
(*He takes the papers from TARTUFFE and hands them to ORGON
as he continues.*)
                Here, they're yours,
Though kept in a seditious cause –

That crime is pardoned. This you owe
To your own *loyalty*, years ago:
During a time of civil war,
It was the King you opted for,
You stood by him, through thick and thin –
This is the way he's always been:
When there's a debt he feels he owes
When least we look for it, he shows
His gratitude, for, while no wrong
Preys on his generous mind for long,
Good offices he does recall
And, in the end, requites them all.

DORINE: Thank Heaven.

MME PERNELLE: I can breathe again.

ELMIRE: I wasn't talking nonsense then –
    I told you things would turn out well.

MARIANE: They stopped the axe before it fell!

ORGON: (*About to lunge at* TARTUFFE.)
    Yooouuu – devious, treacherous...

CLEANTE: Brother, wait!
    Let's leave him to his wretched fate,
    And hope that he'll return one day...

DAMIS: Don't tell me: to the 'middle way'.

CLEANTE: ...while giving thanks to this great prince,
    The best, most merciful of kings.

ORGON: We'll lay our thanks, then, at his feet,
    And, when that business is complete,
    Turn to another, for tonight
    Valère must have what's his by right,
    My daughter, since his love's remained
    So generous, and so...*unfeigned*.

The End.

Appendix
Cléante's speeches in full

*In the National Theatre's production of this text (Spring 2002)
significant cuts were made to two of Cléante's speeches in Act One. The
unabridged versions of these speeches are reproduced below.*

CLEANTE: Your kind
   All talk like that – because you're blind
   You'd rather others didn't see.
   You deem perceptiveness to be
   A kind of sin! Let us adore
   The idols that *you* kneel before
   Or else be damned. Well, listen here:
   Your sermons don't fill *me* with fear,
   I know my subject, for a start
   And Heaven sees into my heart.
   I don't believe your pious pose.
   If there's false courage, then, God knows,
   There is false piety as well:
   The brave man you can always tell
   By how he doesn't rant and roar
   And bluster in the heat of war;
   And how may pious men be known?
   They don't pull faces, sigh and groan.
   D'you really have so dull a wit
   That you can't tell a hypocrite
   From an unfeigned, religious man?
   It doesn't look as though you can –
   You treat them as a single case,
   Confound the visor with the face.
   Sincerity you either miss
   Or else confuse with artifice,
   Substance and air, false coin and true
   Will merge, in your distorted view.
   We humans are a curious lot –
   The fact is, few of us have got

A sense of Nature's golden mean,
We can't keep straight, we have to lean
To one, extreme and dangerous side;
The bounds of reason aren't that wide,
Staying within them is a feat
Beyond our scope – you seldom meet
A man who'll tread its narrow way
If there's a chance for him to stray.
Many a noble cause is wrecked
By charging boldly on, unchecked,
To dizzy uplands of excess,
Where more invariably means less.
(Those last remarks weren't *à propos* –
I felt I had to make them, though.)

ORGON: Oh you're infallible, you are!
　　　Nobody sees so deep or far –
　　　You are a Cato for our age,
　　　An oracle, a mighty sage.
　　　Anyone else is just a prat
　　　Compared to you.

CLEANTE: 　　　　　　I don't think that,
　　　But I know one thing more than you:
　　　I *can* distinguish false from true.
　　　Like the next man, I recognise
　　　Religion as a thing to prize.
　　　What jewel more precious can there be
　　　Than perfect, unfeigned piety,
　　　A fervour that is felt, and real?
　　　But this, this *squashed flea* kind of zeal,
　　　Worn as a lady wears her paint,
　　　The posturing of the plaster saint,
　　　This, above all things, I deplore –
　　　Nothing on earth disgusts me more
　　　Than the religious charlatan,
　　　The ladder-climbing holy man
　　　Whose sanctimonious grimace
　　　Is *donned*, to get some post or place –

I mean the kind of man who's made
Of sacred things a stock in trade.
Religion is his merchandise,
For him, the way to Fortune lies
Through Heaven: are his eyes kept low?
Does he cry out to let you know
How full he is of the Lord's praise?
That's the false coin in which he pays
For influence, or some post he seeks,
He's always praying, when he speaks
Of God, his ardour sounds so pure,
And why? He wants a sinecure!
This is the type of man you'll meet
Preaching seclusion and retreat
While comfortably ensconced at Court,
A hybrid of the vilest sort,
Quick, devious, treacherous, he'll conceal
His viciousness with studied zeal,
He will destroy a man, and claim
That it was done in Heaven's name –
What better way is there to hide
His bitter and resentful pride?
He is more greatly to be feared
Because his weapons are revered,
His fervour's popular, and so
You will hear people cry, 'Bravo!'
As victims perish in the fire
Of his 'just' wrath, his 'righteous' ire.
But if you seek the other kind,
The truly saintly, you will find
They, too, are easy to discern:
They do not seethe, and boil, and burn
With faith that's *too* good to be true,
They hate that sort of ballyhoo.
Nor will you see them rush about
Ferreting so-called sinners out
And damning them – they call that proud,
By them, some licence is allowed,

Humanity shines out of them,
There's only one way they'll condemn
Such actions as they can't condone –
That's by the goodness of their own.
They don't see evil everywhere,
They're more disposed to deem it rare.
They're tolerant of their fellow men,
Nor do they share the zealot's yen
For intrigue. They have just one aim:
To live good lives. They're not aflame
With wrath against us sinners. No,
It's *sin* they hate. They will not go
Further than Heaven means them to
In Heaven's defence. Now, in my view,
These are the truly virtuous,
The models for the rest of us.
Is your man like them? I fear not.
I'd lump him with the other lot;
Your feeling for him's genuine
But you've been badly taken in.

CPSIA information can be obtained
at www.ICGtesting.com
Printed in the USA
JSHW021022220120
3749JS00007B/63